THE
EVERYTHING®

ETIQUETTE
MINI BOOK

Nat Segaloff

A

Adams Media Corporation

Holbrook, Massachusetts

An Everything® Series Book.
"Everything" is a registered trademark of Adams Media Corporation.

Published by Adams Media Corporation
260 Center Street, Holbrook, MA 02343
www.adamsmedia.com

ISBN: 1-58062-499-5

Printed in Canada.

J I H G F E D C B A

Library of Congress Cataloging-in-Publication Data
available from the publisher.

This publication is designed to provide accurate and authoritative information with
regard to the subject matter covered. It is sold with the understanding that the
publisher is not engaged in rendering legal, accounting, or other professional
advice. If legal advice or other expert assistance is required, the services of a
competent professional person should be sought.

— From a *Declaration of Principles* jointly adopted by a Committee of the
American Bar Association and a Committee of Publishers and Associations

Cover illustrations by Barry Littmann.
Interior illustrations by Barry Littmann and Kathie Kelleher.

*This book is available at quantity discounts for bulk purchases.
For information, call 1-800-872-5627.*

See the entire Everything® series at everything.com

Contents

Introduction

Etiquette is widely (though incorrectly) regarded as a social barrier, something that only snobs care about. But simply defined, *etiquette* is the way civilized human beings behave around one another to minimize conflict. It operates under the general assumption that people who interact in a society agree to follow its customs.

But how can you know what custom dictates for every situation? This book covers everything you might run up against in this crazy, exacting world.

As the saying goes, he who asks nicely gets the goods. Following the protocols of etiquette goes a long way, whether you are dealing with your friends or family, or even at important business functions. This engaging little book will not only teach you the rules, but how to follow them in any situation.

Chapter One

R-E-S-P-E-C-T:
Meeting and Greeting

America is a friendly country, sometimes too friendly. Whose business is it if somebody has had an affair or takes an extra Sweet 'N Low packet from a restaurant? In fact, how come there are so many people who don't want so many other people to be allowed to do so much stuff? Maybe all they really need is to have a little respect.

What *is* respect?

Respect is honoring other people and their feelings. "I try to be aware of my neighbors," says a lady who lives in a large, impersonal apartment complex in a big city. "For example, whenever I see elderly persons in the hall, I always smile and say hello to them. It seems minor, but so many old people live alone that I may be the only person all day who says anything to them." *That's* respect.

It's also allowing people to live their own lives, and living one's own life so as to not infringe on the lives of others. It's the belief that, "My right to swing my fist ends where your nose begins." Finally, it's people having enough faith in their own way of living that another person's way of living doesn't threaten them. Etiquette shows us how to reach this level.

Forms of Address

Unless a formal title of royal, political, or religious office dictates otherwise, ordinary men and women are referred to in the following ways in conversation and correspondence:

- *Mr.* Men over the age of 18.
- *Messrs.* Two or more brothers with the same last name. This designation is not used for father, son, or people with different last names, such as law firm partners.
- *Miss.* Unmarried women in years past were addressed this way, but "Ms." (pronounced "Miz") has come to be accepted in formal matters. "Miss" is still appropriate for girls under 16.
- *Mrs.* A married woman uses her husband's name, as in "Mrs. Elmer Davies," not "Mrs. Gertrude Davies."
- *Ms.* Can be used for any woman, either by her request or when her marital status is not known.

Younger people still should call older people "Sir" or "Ma'am." If the older person wants to be called otherwise, he or she will say so. On the other hand, an older person calling a younger person "Sir" or "Ma'am" is awkward and, depending on vocal inflection, can be an insult.

Only people of the same age, or whose relationship has become informal, may, with mutual consent only, properly use each other's first names.

Addressing Professionals

Nothing is more disconcerting than a patient calling her physician "Dr. Miller" while he calls her "Judy." Imagine if she then said, "How ya doin', Steve?"

It is inappropriate for a doctor to call his or her patient by a first name unless the patient permits it. Likewise, it should always be "Dr. Miller" from the patient unless, of course, there is a friendship that predates the professional relationship. These rules apply to all other professional relationships.

Married Name Versus Unmarried Name

Although the term *maiden name* is becoming obsolete, the question remains whether a newly married woman will continue to be addressed by her former name or will acquire her husband's.

Whichever she chooses, it is her obligation to make her choice known, either through a line in the formal wedding announcement ("The bride will continue to use her unmarried name of Sloan"), on her business card, or, more rarely, on her calling card. She should also reintroduce herself by her chosen name to those who knew her before her nuptials. If she does not do so, others are correct in believing she has assumed her husband's last name.

Children's Last Names

Any teacher who reads a class roster has had to deal with the extraordinary assortment of hyphenated and nonmatching names brought about by family change. Divorced mothers may resume using their maiden names whereas their children retain the mother's married name (Scott Gross, son of Susan Fricke and James Gross). Parents may hyphenate their last names and give them to their child (Justin Smith-Menz, son of Edie Smith and Thomas Menz).

However, a child living with her remarried mother may not assume her stepfather's last name unless she has been formally adopted by him (Meagan Meadows, daughter of Sam and

Shirley [née Graham] Peterson). The designation née means "born as" and is used to indicate a married woman's former, unmarried (née: maiden) name.

Addressing Ph.D.s

The degree of doctor of philosophy is one whose holder deserves respect and usually asks for it by appending the term *Doctor* to his or her name, as in "Dr. Pretorius." One who holds an honorary doctorate may still be called doctor.

Visiting

Sleepovers

When staying as a guest in someone else's house, you are expected to respect the moral beliefs of the host. This means that sleeping arrangements should be determined in advance of the visit or at least well before retiring on the first evening.

Unmarried guests should not put their host in the position of making a moral judgment. If the host directs unmarried guests to separate bedrooms, this is more than a hint but less than a command. Where host and guest are good friends, of course, such questions have long since been settled.

Couples (married or unmarried) involved in a physical relationship may enjoy having sex in new places. If that place happens to be some-body else's house, they should be discreet about it. It is also improper for a hostess to inquire after her guests' sex life.

Gifts for a Hostess or Host

Overnight guests enjoying the hospitality of a friend or relative should bring a house gift with them for the host or hostess. This can be anything from a bottle of good wine to a coffee table book. Toys for young children or remembrances for older children or other relatives living in the house will likewise be well regarded.

An additional way to show appreciation is for guests to take their host family out to dinner at least once during the stay.

Guest of Honor

If a house guest is to be feted by his host, the guest of honor should send flowers or a centerpiece to the home, timed to arrive before the party.

Guest Towels

Guests, when using the host's lavatory, should not use the host's personal bath towels. They should use—and the host must provide—

separate cloth guest towels. A roll of paper towels will not do. If there has been any splashing in the lavatory, the guest should restore the cleanliness of the room before leaving it.

Smokers in a Nonsmoking Home

Smoking guests should refrain absolutely from smoking in a nonsmoking home.

If (when) smokers must light up, they should do so outdoors, preferably far enough from the house that their breath and clothing can air out before they step back inside. Most nonsmokers are offended by the lingering aroma of tobacco, even a friend's.

Nonsmokers in a Smoker's Home

Smokers may, out of courtesy, refrain from smoking when nonsmokers are guests in their house. It hardly matters, anyway, because their curtains, rugs, and upholstery already smell of smoke.

This can pose a family problem when out-of-town relatives refuse to remain under a smoker's roof. If this happens, the guest may explain exactly why he is staying in a hotel: "It's not you, it's your smoking."

Serving Alcohol

The heightened awareness of alcoholism and other substance abuse has made the general public more sensitive, in some cases overly so, about serving alcohol at social gatherings. A host or hostess is responsible for the safety of his or her guests, and this includes allowing them to overindulge. The wise host knows his own limits and stays sober to monitor the limits of others. If a guest appears to be losing control, the host should take all steps to cut him off from the bar or to take him aside and insist that he refrain, sleep it off, or leave in a taxi.

Alcoholics

Anyone who has acknowledged his or her dependency on alcohol and has joined Alcoholics Anonymous (AA) (or another program) should be respected. Too often, though, other people will assume that they may not drink, or even mention alcohol, around a friend who is a recovering alcoholic. It then becomes a burden on the part of the AA member to put everybody else at ease.

It is perfectly all right to serve alcohol at a gathering where one or more members may be in a program, provided, of course, that you provide nonalcoholic alternatives.

A person who does not care to drink *for whatever reason* should simply say, "No thank you, I don't want a drink." No one has the right to ask, or assume, why.

Let Sleeping Guests Lie

It is courteous to allow out-of-town guests to "sleep in" if they are visiting on vacation. This does not mean, however, that the host must reschedule his life around that of the person using the spare bedroom. Establish schedules in advance. For example, if four people have to use the bathroom in the morning, the guest may want to catch half an hour of extra z's.

Guest Safety

Hosts are obliged to indicate to their guests the nearest exit, where the first aid kit and fire extinguisher are, and what number to call for a doctor. Hosts in earthquake-prone areas might also advise guests on what to do if the earth moves (such as to keep shoes nearby, stand under the door frame, and use the flashlight that's kept under the bed).

Unannounced Guests

A host is under no obligation to see guests who drop in without calling ahead, or who phone from the car and announce that they happen to be in the neighborhood. Depending upon whether the host wants to receive the callers, he can stretch dinner portions, delay his own plans, or make new and inclusive ones. It is grossly rude to expect to be welcomed into a home that is not expecting you.

Residential Phone Etiquette

The telephone is a convenience that is often used inconveniently. In general, a ringing telephone should be answered, but there is nothing wrong with telling the caller that you haven't got time for an extended conversation now and asking him or her to call back later. Remember that the phone is an invention, not an excuse.

Unless you are familiar with someone's sleep habits, it is best to restrict residential phone calls to between 8 A.M. and 10 P.M. on weekdays, 10 A.M. and 10 P.M. on Saturdays, and noon and 10 P.M. on Sundays. Some people, particularly those who have known recent tragedy, come to regard wee-hours phone calls as harbingers of bad news.

An awareness of television programming and sports events is also helpful; phoning during *The X Files* or "sudden death" in NBA playoffs may be actionable in some social circles!

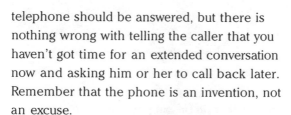

Never make phone calls when intoxicated. The slang name for this is "having the dialies." If you receive a call from a friend who is obviously in an altered state, first ascertain if there is a legitimate problem and, if there isn't, request that he or she phone back during normal hours. Any conversation conducted under such circumstances is likely to be embarrassing the next morning for one or both parties.

Ten Commandments of House Guests

Guests enjoying overnight hospitality with friends incur certain obligations toward their host. In general, the tenet of good guest behavior is, "Except when they see you, you're never there."

1. Guests should neatly maintain their accommodations (whether a pull-out sofa bed in

the living room or a full private bungalow) and not scatter their belongings all over the house.

2. Unless there is maid service (yeah, right), guests should make their own beds every morning until the morning they depart.

3. Remove personal toiletries from the bathroom after each use (unless it's your private bathroom).

4. Make sure the seat of the john is always down.

5. Don't use the phone without asking permission, and then don't tie it up. Use your own long-distance account, not your host's.

6. Treat the host's children, pets, friends, and property with respect.

7. Conform to the host's schedule; don't ask them to cancel their plans or eat an hour earlier or later.

8. Always ask whether the host needs help in the kitchen, in cleaning up, in repairing anything, in sharing driving, and so on.

9. If you break something, tell the host right away, and then deal with it.

10. Have firm arrival and, more important, departure times; remember Benjamin Franklin's exhortation that fish and house guests begin to smell after three days.

Neighborliness

New Neighbors

It's been decades since local merchants dispatched a "welcome wagon" to greet arrivals to a residential neighborhood. Nowadays the salutation seems to be, "Hey, buddy, how long are you gonna park your damn U-Haul here?" Although the American

credo seems to be "avoid thy neighbor," in fact a lot of potential conflicts could be forestalled or eliminated entirely by simply saying hello to the people who live nearby. Neighborhoods change, no doubt about it. Long-time residents pine for the days when families lived where students now dwell. Much of what passes for malice is just ignorance: new neighbors not knowing the values of the block they're moving into. Suburban kids who migrate to city apartments may not be aware that they can't play the stereo loud any more; that the local custom is to safeguard parking spaces; that trash collection isn't free and they can't just chuck stuff into anybody's garbage can; and so forth.

Housewarming Gifts. Despite these cynical times, new neighbors may appreciate token gifts when they move in. Something as simple as a few bottles of chilled spring water on moving day, or a list of nearby merchants (supermarket, laundromat, drug store, hardware store, service station, dry cleaner, and so forth) can be enormously helpful.

Pets

A dog that barks incessantly or a cat in heat next door can be annoying. Too often, a pet owner has no idea of the noise his animal makes when he's gone, even though the rest of the neighborhood does. Pet owners should monitor their animals (a cassette recorder with a "voice-activated" feature can help) to make sure that they are not creating a neighborhood disturbance.

If a dog is disturbing you regularly, asking, "Is there anything you can do about your pet? His barking is keeping me up" is a safe place to start. If the problem continues, you may have to phone the overworked animal control officer at your local police department. If there is a question of an animal being mistreated, call the American Humane Association or the Society for the Prevention of Cruelty to Animals.

Most communities have leash laws, and, even if they don't, no community sanctions pet owners whose animals relieve themselves on a neighbor's lawn.

Loud Parties

People living in crowded residential areas who are planning large parties have a special responsibility not to let the celebration get out of hand. Most communities forbid noises after 10 P.M. or before 7 A.M.

In cities, student areas, and condominium complexes where proximity makes the noise problem worse, some precautions may be taken:

1. Keep the party indoors.
2. Hire security guards.
3. Invite your immediate neighbors to the party. Even if they decline, they will feel more involved and will be less apt to complain.
4. Set a clear end time, and let the neighbors know what it's going to

be. Let your guests know it, too, and enforce it.

5. Invite no more people than you can handle.

If this seems too restrictive, then perhaps the party should take place in a more suitable venue.

Family Noises

Noisy kids, domestic "disagreements," and cataclysmic passion should stay within the home of the family having them. The sounds from those and other activities, however, sometimes stray from house to house or, more commonly, from apartment to apartment. Curiosity may have killed the cat, but it can give a neighbor some wrong ideas.

Parking Easements

The shared alley space between two adjacent houses is called an "easement," and it should remain clear and easily navigable, both as a courtesy and for fire vehicle access. Those who do not honor their neighbor's right-of-way not only are thoughtless but also may be violating the law.

Garbage

Neighbors have a responsibility to maintain securely locking garbage containers that leak neither odor nor contents.

Housewarming Gifts

Friends invited to housewarming parties can help by bringing household items, but it would be improper to throw a housewarming party in lieu of making a trip to the hardware store. Since most people usually require new kitchenware after they move, some possible gifts are:

- Canister set
- Coffee or tea
- Dish drainer
- Doormat
- Kitchen gadgets (peeler, grater, etc.)
- Kitchen towels
- Place mats and napkins
- Plants
- Spice rack
- Sponges and cleaning supplies
- Strainer, colander
- Wine glasses (everyday)

Religious Caveats

Visiting a Church as the Guest of a Parishioner

Religion is one of three subjects that divide people (the other two being politics and, as we discovered, etiquette). Yet if one attends services of a faith different from one's own, one is expected to respond with courtesy.

Some religions, notably Mormon, do not permit nonmembers to attend sacred services. Outsiders also may be excluded from certain Islamic observances. Still other religions forbid their own members to attend services of competing faiths.

As a general rule, guests are not expected to participate in religious activities that run contrary to their beliefs. Respectful silence is the best behavior.

Discussions of One's Religion

Etiquette has a unique position on religion: *none*. Just as it is not proper to inquire after someone's religion, so it is not proper to force one's religion on someone else. Some sects believe that the proselytizing of their beliefs is not only sanctioned by Scripture but also divinely blessed. They should understand that others do not share their beliefs and, in fact, often resent them.

As etiquette seeks to avoid conflict rather than arbitrate it, the best response to someone who tries to impose his religion on you is to say, "No, thank you." Just as society considers it repulsive for someone to eat with his hands, tell vulgar jokes, or have bad hygiene, so does society disapprove of people who force their idea of God upon those who do not wish to share it. Such people also usually feel that God instructs them to supersede human laws in spreading His. In America this is a question best settled by the Constitution, not etiquette.

Political Stands

As one of the Big Three divisive subjects, politics are out of place in an otherwise nonpartisan social gathering. There are reasons why lapel pins are not considered part of formal attire; neither are armbands, sashes, or AIDS ribbons, no matter how valid the cause. Historically, politics were discussed after dinner in the library over brandy and cigars—and by men only. While mores have changed, human sensitivity over politics has not.

Campaign Placards

Whether on lawns, windows, or bumpers, political campaign signs are a patriotic American right—no matter how much of a scoundrel the politician might be! As political speech, campaign signs enjoy full protection under the Bill of Rights. Landlords and condo associations may not remove them from a tenant's window or levy a penalty for displaying them.

Just Plain Rude

Nakedness

Although the human body may be a temple, not everybody wants to worship there. Nudity not only is inappropriate but also can be offensive, even illegal, when people are not expecting it.

Therefore, guests in others' houses, people in their own houses with guests present, girls and boys on senior class trips, or anyone answering the door should do so fully clothed unless all parties are of an age to consent and have consented.

Wolf Whistles

Women do not consider it a compliment to be whistled at, whether from street level, above it, or below it. Men (for they are not gentlemen) who do so demean themselves, not the lady.

Chapter Two

Good Form: The Written Word

Anyone who has ever gotten a form letter, or tried to decide which fork to use, or wanted to know if purple was okay for a cummerbund, knows how frustrating, even maddening, convention can be. Trouble is, some societal baselines are essential.

The best way to write letters is to just pick up a pen and paper and do it. The gift of a letter, and the importance such a gesture means to a lasting friendship, cannot be overstated. The very act of touching a sheet of paper that a friend has also touched can strengthen the bond between them. Even when it's an engraved invitation, a typed letter, or the product of a word processor, there is, well, a *substance* in a letter that cannot even be approached by the transience of a phone call. This is why society has developed guidelines, not only in writing but in other endeavors.

Stationery

Personal and Business Correspondence

Tradition exists surrounding paper, envelopes, number of folds, color of ink, borders, and how correspondence is inserted and sealed. Fortunately, custom has eased since the days when replies to formal invitations had to be written in black or blue ink on white or ivory paper, and notes had to be sent on engraved rather than merely printed letterhead.

One caveat: writing etiquette is now in service of the U.S. Postal Service as to envelope size, position of address, and clarity of printing.

Basic Stationery

The following presents the most common types of stationery and their purpose:

Foldover cards. Used for informal notes, they measure 4" × 5" when folded (8" × 5" flat) and have matching envelopes. There is a monogram on the very top of the front page and a return address on the back flap of the envelope.

Personal stationery. Used for letters, sheets measure 7" × 9" and bear the sender's full name, address, and phone number printed vertically at the top; additional pages are blank pages of the same paper. Matching envelopes are for a one-third fold.

Business stationery. Sheets measure 8½" × 11" with name, address, and phone number printed vertically at the top (there is some allowance for artistic layout). Matching No. 10 envelopes are for a one-third fold.

Post cards. Used for quick notes, they measure approximately 4" × 6" on heavy card stock printed with colored border and the sender's name only on the top. These can also quite properly be sent in matching envelopes.

Memo pads. Single or bound ("perfect binding"), they measure anywhere from one-third of a page to one-quarter of a page, are printed with "Memo" on the top and the sender's name on the bottom. Use of the phrase "from the desk of" or "stuff I thought of" (or anything else) is considered tacky. Quite often memos are attached to other documents in lieu of writing a cover letter.

Celebrities frequently choose stationery with either their name or address (but not both) printed on the envelope to avoid extra eyes learning their address. A single woman may also properly use only her address, and not her name, on the return address printed on an envelope.

Businesses, of course, may have far more elaborate stationery carrying corporate logos, subsidiaries, names of their board of directors or ranking counsel, international offices, and so on.

Inappropriate Stationery

One should never mix business and pleasure, at least not in writing. Personal use of business stationery may reflect on the business itself and, in addition, may offend the recipient who is due a strictly personal note.

It is also incorrect, not to mention hurtful, for a businessperson to have a secretary type personal correspondence. Many is the child who has been distanced from his or her "too busy" parent by such a practice.

Finally, one should never return a letter to its sender by writing on it with the excuse of saving time and paper, even though the government and some mail order companies employ the practice. A letter of request requires a separate and complete reply. The only exception would be a contract or a writer's manuscript where emendations are required by the nature of the transaction.

Greeting Cards

Despite advertising claims, a prewritten, mass-produced commercial greeting card is never as personal or appreciated as an individual letter. The proof is that nobody looks on the back of a letter to see how much you spent for it.

Commercial greeting cards can be ornate or clever. Some even play music or sound like cows. But they aren't letters.

It helps take the onus off of using commercial greeting cards to add a handwritten note to the blank side facing the printed message. The only part of a personal note that may be typed is the envelope (out of respect for the post office).

Writing Personal Letters on a Computer

Formal letters must be written only by hand. Modern technology, however, has made it increasingly acceptable—and certainly faster and easier—to write personal letters on word processors or e-mail, and even to fax them instead of mailing them. It's a tough call; strictly speaking, it is a shame to take the personal touch (literally) out of correspondence. On the other hand (also literally), a letter written on a computer is better than none at all.

Dual Signatures

When one member of a couple writes a letter for both of them, only the actual writer signs it. Postcards, telegrams, and gift cards may be signed by both parties.

First Name Versus Full Name

Business letters are signed with a person's full name unless a friendship or informality exists between the sender and recipient. One should not sign only one's first name as a means of ingratiating or obligating a recipient whom one does not know.

Married women signing business letters should sign them by the name with which they conduct business, such as "Eleanor Botkin." If she is signing a business letter concerning a matter involving both herself and her husband, she may sign "Eleanor Botkin (Mrs. George Sand)."

Personal letters, of course, are signed with one's first name. Additional guidelines on signatures can be found in numerous books and guides, as well as in the back of office dictionaries.

Invitations and Announcements

Sample Engagement Announcement for a Newspaper

The following are examples of engagement announcements to a newspaper.

Mr. and Mrs. Adam Claypool of Hillandale, Maryland, announce the engagement of their daughter, Miss Justine Claypool, to Mr. James Brendan Danielson of Dallas, Texas. Mr. Danielson is the son of Dr. and Mrs. Roger Wakefield Danielson, also of Dallas. A November wedding is planned.

Miss Claypool is a graduate of the University of Maryland and is a development executive for National Public Radio. Mr. Danielson is a graduate of the Rochester Institute of Technology and is a biochemist with the Naval Ordinance Laboratory.

SALLY LOUISE SMITH
TO WED JOHN F. JONES

Mr. and Mrs. Harvey Smith of Palmersville announce the engagement of their daughter, Sally Louise, to John F. Jones of Waynesville. The couple will be married on November 1.

Miss Smith is a graduate of Palmersville High School and the Choate Academy and holds a B.A. in Art History. She is an instructor at the Museum School.

Mr. Jones, son of Mr. and Mrs. Chester H. Jones, earned his Bachelor's degree from Hunt College and his law degree from Scott University. He is an associate in the firm of Dewey, Cheetham, and Howe.

A photograph of the bride-to-be may accompany the release.

Sample Wedding Announcement for a Newspaper

A wedding announcement to a newspaper can read as follows:

Mr. and Mrs. Adam Claypool of Hillandale, Maryland, announce the marriage of their daughter, Justine, to Mr. James Brendan Danielson of Dallas, Texas. Mr. Danielson is the son of Dr. and Mrs. Roger Wakefield Danielson, also of Dallas.

The bride, who will retain her last name of Claypool, is a graduate of the University of Maryland and is a development executive for National Public Radio. The groom was graduated from the Rochester Institute of Technology and is a biochemist with the Naval Ordinance Laboratory.

The couple will reside in Bethesda, Maryland.

Wedding Invitations

Given all combinations of married, widowed, and divorced parents, plus the wedding details, there are many variations on standard invitations and announcements. A wedding consultant can compose one that fits the particulars, but here are those that occur most often. The basic wedding invitation is quite formal:

Mr. and Mrs. Adam Claypool
request the honour of your presence
at the marriage of their daughter
Justine
to
Mr. James Brendan Danielson
on Friday, the ninth of November
Two thousand and one
at twelve o'clock [or: noon]
Church of Our Savior
Hillandale, Maryland

Notice the British spelling of *honour* and the complete spelling of numbers, except for long addresses, which would be awkward. Use of *Miss* also is generally reserved for invitations sent by the bride herself or where she has no relatives. There is no punctuation save for the period after *Mr.* or *Mrs.* The invitation is engraved on fine card stock, enclosed in an inner envelope on which the recipients' names are written by hand in black ink only, and enclosed in a larger envelope for mailing. The mailing envelope, too, is addressed in ink by hand, preferably by someone skilled in calligraphy.

Where a recipient may also be invited to a reception following the wedding ceremony, a separate and smaller card is enclosed:

Reception immediately following the ceremony
Red Rim Country Club
Briggs-Chaney Road
Hillandale
The favour of a reply is requested
594 Beacon Road, Silver Spring, Maryland 20903

If the wedding ceremony has been private,
guests may be invited to the reception only:

Mr. and Mrs. Adam Claypool
request the pleasure of your company
at the wedding reception of their daughter
Justine
and
Mr. James Brendan Danielson
on Friday, the ninth of November
Two thousand and one
at one o'clock
Red Rim Country Club . . .

There are numerous permutations that address such issues as divorced parents of the bride, divorced parents of the groom, one or more deceased parents of either the bride or groom, divorced and one remarried parent of either, or someone other than a parent giving the bride away. Here is an assortment of wordings (courtesy of *The Everything® Wedding Book* by Janet Anastasio and Michelle Bevilacqua); a wedding consultant can also specify which is appropriate.

When both the bride's and groom's parents sponsor the wedding:

Mr. and Mrs. Roger Parker
and
Mr. and Mrs. Robert Clark
request the honour of your presence
at the marriage of their children
Beth Elaine Parker
and
Mr. Justin James Clark
on Saturday, the fifth of August
Two thousand and one
at two o'clock
Center Street Baptist Church
Fairview, Pennsylvania

When the groom's parents sponsor the wedding:

Mr. and Mrs. Robert Clark
request the honour of your presence
at the marriage of
Beth Elaine Parker
to their son
Mr. Justin James Clark . . .

When the bride and groom sponsor their own wedding:

The honour of your presence is requested
at the marriage of
Miss Beth Elaine Parker
and
Mr. Justin James Clark . . .

When the mother of the bride is sponsoring and has not remarried:

Mrs. James Parker
requests the honour of your presence
at the marriage of her daughter
Beth Elaine Parker . . .

When the mother of the bride is sponsoring and has remarried:

> *Mrs. David C. Hayes*
> *requests the honour of your presence*
> *at the marriage of her daughter*
> *Beth Elaine Parker . . .*

When the mother of the bride has remarried and she is sponsoring the wedding with her husband, who has not adopted her daughter:

> *Mr. and Mrs. David C. Hayes*
> *request the honour of your presence*
> *at the marriage of Mrs. Hayes's daughter*
> *Beth Elaine Parker . . .*

When the father of the bride is sponsoring
and has not remarried:

Mr. Roger Parker
requests the honour of your presence
at the marriage of his daughter
Beth Elaine . . .

When the father of the bride has remarried
and is sponsoring:

Mr. and Mrs. Roger Parker
request the honour of your presence
at the marriage of Mr. Parker's daughter
Beth Elaine . . .

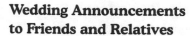

Wedding Announcements to Friends and Relatives

An announcement of the nuptials may be sent after the fact to people who, for whatever reason, were not invited to the ceremony itself:

Mr. and Mrs. Adam Claypool

and

Dr. and Mrs. Roger Wakefield

announce the marriage of

Justine Claypool

and

Mr. James Brendan Danielson

on Friday, the ninth of November

Two thousand and one

Hillandale, Maryland

Wedding Shower Invitations

Although handwritten notes are preferred, preprinted invitation cards are being used with increasing frequency. As long as the host and mode of gift are stated, there is no problem:

Dear Rebecca,

Margaret Weitz and I are hosting a wedding shower for Pam Matthews on Sunday, August 3, at 4 P.M. at my house. She and Ron are registered at Bloomingdale's and Crate and Barrel, and Margaret and I are also keeping track of who's giving what in the "major gift" department, if it's at all helpful to you.

We look forward to seeing you here on the third. Let me know if you can come.

Sincerely,

R.S.V.P. 555-2345

Baby Shower Invitations

These can be quite informal, but still require written notice. Of course, they apply to the first baby only, as the second baby is showered with the hand-me-downs of the first baby, if gender allows. They are hosted by friends:

Come to Mary Litwak's Baby Shower!
on
Sunday, September 23 at 4 P.M.
at
416 Niemann Place, Apartment 6, Cornishtown
R.S.V.P. Cindy Memelstein, 555-5545

A notation about gifts can be added at the bottom of the card (in handwriting if it is printed).

Birth Announcements

Commercial announcements can be formal, in which a small card bearing the newborn's name is tied with ribbon to a larger one showing the parents' names:

Small card:

> *Charlotte Ann MacGregor*
> *March 25, 2001*

Tied to a bigger card:

> *Mr. and Mrs. Addison MacGregor*
> *49 Shawn Drive*
> *Wheaton, MD 20902*

To the less formal (single card):

> *Our Home Has New Joy!*
> *Name: Charlotte Ann MacGregor*
> *Weight: Six pounds, ten ounces*
> *Length: Twenty inches*
>
> *Carole and Addison MacGregor*
> *49 Shawn Drive*
> *Wheaton, MD 20902*

It is especially appropriate to announce adoptions:

> *Mr. and Mrs. Addison MacGregor*
> *are pleased to announce the adoption of*
> *James Michael*
> *Age: eighteen months*

Child's Birthday Party Invitations

There are tons of commercially printed, festive invitations for kids' parties. They are sent to the child in care of the parent (mother):

Please come to Shelley's Fifth Birthday!
on Saturday, April 19, at 4 P.M.
at Showcase Shake 'n' Pizza
6556 Glendale Parkway
Glendale, California
R.S.V.P. to Shelley's Mom (Wendi), 555-6666
Ice cream, cake, and pizza

Anniversary Party Invitations

Formal anniversary observances (at 25 or 50 years) may be grand events with hired ballrooms and orchestras, or they can be friends and family. The situation dictates the invitation, as does the host of the celebration:

1976–2001
Mr. and Mrs. Paul Frederick
request the pleasure of your company
at a reception honoring their
silver wedding anniversary
Sunday, October 18, at 7:30 P.M.
Bombay Yacht Club
R.S.V.P. 3601 Connecticut Avenue, NW

An invitation sent by children might read:

1951–2001
Buddy Frederick and Celia Frederick Collins
invite you to honor their parents
Mr. and Mrs. Paul Frederick
on the occasion of their
golden wedding anniversary
Saturday, October 18, at 7:30 P.M.
Bombay Yacht Club
R.S.V.P. 286 Ashdown Street (Buddy)

Christening and Baptism Invitations

Christening invitations are kept informal (as for the Jewish circumcision) as they occur so quickly after the child's birth. A phone call or handwritten note will suffice, although printed invitations are certainly correct.

Dear Kietryn and Keith,

Our adorable Becky is being christened on Sunday at St. Ambrose's at 2 P.M. We would love for you to join us and come back to the house afterward for a light buffet.

Yours truly,

First Communions

There is no formal invitation for a communion. Phone calls and notes may advise friends and relatives of the occasion beforehand. The post-communion party is generally attended as a group by the girls, boys, their parents, and

godparents, all of whom have just celebrated
their first Communion.

Bar Mitzvah Invitations

Mr. and Mrs. Samuel Snyder
invite you to the
Bar Mitzvah of their son
Edward Amram
Saturday, November 23
at 10 o'clock in the morning
at the
Congregation Jacob Ben Utz
6600 Galway Boulevard
Shaker Heights, Ohio
R.S.V.P.
10406 Fawcett Avenue
Shaker Heights, Ohio

Marriage Vow Renewal Invitations

The couple electing to renew their wedding vows will send out their own invitations, which can be informal (handwritten) or formal, but more usually informal:

Donna and Buddy Joe Becker
request the honor of your presence
as they renew their marriage vows
on the occasion of their
tenth wedding anniversary
Thursday, May 18, at 6 P.M.
Christ Church, Cambridge
R.S.V.P.
555-1667
Reception following the ceremony
at the Church meeting room

Second Baptism Invitations

There is no general precedent for a formal invitation to an Evangelical Baptism at which one embraces Jesus Christ as Lord and becomes "born again." An informal or tele-phoned invitation may be extended, although a handwritten one is appropriate:

Praise God
and witness the rebirth in Christ of
Jean James Munson
at the Church of the Holy Redeemer
on Sunday, February 2, at noon
Reception afterward in
Church family room
R.S.V.P. 555-1122

Invitations with Strings Attached

When the purpose of throwing a party is to raise rent, solicit charitable contributions, sell plastic food containers, hawk cosmetics, or anything other than to celebrate, this must be disclosed to the guests when they are invited.

The same holds for B.Y.O.B. (bring your own bottle) or B.Y.O.F. (bring your own food/pot luck) gatherings. It is especially true for bachelor or bachelorette parties held in expensive venues where those attending may be asked to ante more than their means will allow. No one should feel pressured into attending a party that, in essence, he or she has to help throw!

Acknowledgments

Formal Reply: R.S.V.P.

R.S.V.P. is a notice that the host or hostess requests a response indicating whether an invited guest will attend the function. A reply is mandatory as soon as the invitation is received to allow the host or hostess to set plans.

Accepting Informal Invitations

An acceptance repeats the pertinent information so that there is no misunderstanding:

Dear Linda,

Scott and I gladly accept your luncheon invitation for Tuesday, December 3, at your home at noon. We look forward to seeing you and Earl again.

Kind regards,

Susan

A similar message also is sent for regrets, again so that there is no misunderstanding:

Dear Linda,

    I am so sorry, but Scott and I already have plans for Tuesday, December 3, and so won't be able to join you and Earl for noon lunch. I hope we'll be able to see each other another time soon.

    Kind regards,

    Susan

Accepting Formal Invitations

As with an informal invitation, a formal invitation demands a response. Often there will be a response card enclosed with the invitation, a sad, but pragmatic, commentary on the times.

Formal responses can be letters:

Dear Mrs. Southwaite:

    Mr. Bradford and I will be honored to join you
and Mr. Chumley at your home for dinner on
Tuesday, December 8, at 7 o'clock.

    We look forward to seeing you then.

    Sincerely,

    Susan Crumb

    (Mrs. Scott Bradford)

They may also be a repeat of the invitation,
except with the word "regret" added:

Mr. and Mrs. Scott Bradford regret that they will
be unable to accept the invitation of Mr. and Mrs.
Earl Chumley on Tuesday, December 8, at 7 o'clock
at 1616 Beverly Boulevard.

Acknowledging Gifts, Cards, and Deeds

Although one may say "thanks" in person (such as when receiving a gift or leaving a dinner party), it is always proper to repeat those thanks in writing immediately after someone has done something nice. The person who accepts another's generosity without thanking him or her for it is, very simply, unworthy of receiving more.

Invitation to a Formal Dinner Party

An invitation to a formal dinner party can read as follows:

Mr. and Mrs. Nutley Rose
request your presence at dinner
to honor Judge and Mrs. William Winship
at eight o'clock on Thursday, July 5
103 Ames Drive
Rockville, Idaho
R.S.V.P.
Formal dress
555-1212

Bread-and-Butter Notes

A thank-you letter sent to a hostess after attending a dinner, or after staying over in her house, is sometimes referred to as a "bread-and-butter note." It needn't be elaborate, but it must be sent (on personal stationery):

Dear Gladys,

Tom and I had a marvelous time with you and Jim last night. Your meal was sumptuous, and the company was equally nourishing. I don't know how you manage to make us feel at home and to do it all so easily! I'll phone in a few days to invite you and Jim over to our house. I can't wait!

Sincerely,
Ruth

It is essential that the guest of honor at a dinner send written thanks.

Positive Letters of Reference

A letter of reference reflects on its writer as well as its subject and should be considered a public document. Although, in modern times, a telephone call by a prospective employer to a former one often substitutes for a letter of reference, it may be convenient to put it in writing.

To Whom It May Concern:

Mary Reilly has been my faithful household employee for many years. During that time she has proved herself industrious, efficient, and, above all, trustworthy. I am forced to let her go at this time because my living situation has changed and she is redundant to the household, but I lose her knowing that whoever employs her will be engaging someone of extraordinary skill and discretion. I trust that person shall be you.

Sincerely,

Henry Jekyll, M.D.

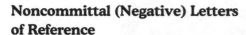

Noncommittal (Negative) Letters of Reference

Unlike a positive recommendation, a negative letter of reference is as notable for what it does not say as for what it does say. It must be neither libelous nor misleading, yet clear enough so that the reader should get the picture without having it drawn for him. Be positive but vague; it is preferable to damn with faint praise than to praise with faint damns.

To Whom It May Concern:

Uriah Heap was in the employ of my firm for several years, and he ably performed his duties throughout the entire time. My business partner and I were no longer able to use his services.

Sincerely,

Philip Pirrup

Letters of Introduction

The formal letter of introduction introduces someone you know to someone else you know, although the two of them do not know each other. Such a letter is, in effect, a blank check drawn against your good reputation and should never be written lightly.

Such letters establish a connection, tell a bit about the person, and subtly acknowledge an obligation in both directions. A copy should be given to both parties:

Dear Pierce,

My writing partner, Betty Crawford, is moving to Columbus with her family where she will be finishing her latest book and accompanying her husband, Tom, who is starting with the Zigler Agency.

Both Betty and Tom are great friends of Cynthia and mine, as are you and Chelsea, and I would dearly appreciate it if you could help them make early contacts in the new city.

I appreciate your time and look forward to seeing you and your family this summer at the beach.

Sincerely,
Ellen Wilkins

Writing to Strangers

Writing to a Celebrity

No celebrity is required to respond to any correspondence that does not pertain directly to his or her work. Many choose to do so because they are aware that their fame depends on their continued favor with the public.

Some must go to considerable trouble and expense sending autographed photos (in the case of retired or cult figures, this can involve financial sacrifice). If writing to a celebrity one should be brief and benign. If you send something to be autographed, include a self-addressed, stamped envelope for its return.

Writing to a Politician

Correspondence with an elected official is likely to be handled by his or her staff and will usually provoke a form letter that barely answers your inquiry. Of course, it differs depending on the individual politician. Generally speaking, however, politicians respond to (without necessarily *answering*) all reasonable correspondence.

Writing to Companies

Writing a company, requesting brochures, filing complaints, commending an employee's good deed, summarizing an agreement reached during a phone call, and ordering merchandise are only a few reasons to write a stranger. This is sometimes called a "cold" letter, meaning that it comes with no prior relationship.

Be clear. The mistake that most people make is, quite literally, to start at the second paragraph. When writing, first *tell the recipient what the letter is going to be about*. Then say it. Then suggest how you might like to resolve the matter. Then say goodbye. For example:

Dear Mr. Mendez:

An encounter with one of your sales clerks yesterday has left me uneasy over the way your bookstore treated me.

I was having trouble finding a particular book and asked a man, whose name tag identified him as Mr. Smith, where the philosophy section was. He told me it was on the lower floor. I asked him where the store directory was, and he said that the directory was on the lower floor, too. My response was to ask why the store doesn't have a

directory on the second floor as well to prevent customers like me from having to climb the stairs every time we want to know something. Mr. Smith replied that I should have looked before I went upstairs.

There are two issues here: first, is Mr. Smith paid to help customers or to lecture them? Second, why don't you have directories on both levels? As far as I am concerned, you could ameliorate both problems with an apology.

Sincerely,

J. Hegelius

Salutations

"Dear Mr. Gable" sounds a little presumptuous for a business letter, especially between two men, but tradition insists it is nevertheless correct.

There are only three other forms, each less acceptable: "My Dear Mr. Gable" sounds condescending; "Dear Clark Gable" or just plain

"Clark Gable" are both cold; and "Dear Sir" is rude, as the letter is addressed to Mr. Gable.

General letters to unknown people that begin "Dear Sir," "Dear Sir or Madam," "Gentlemen," "Ladies," "Dear Friend," or some other vague vocative (from the Latin *to call*) also are improper. Even "To Whom It May Concern" is dicey and impersonal, if useful. And "Dear Credit Manager" is pushing it. If you don't know to whom you're writing, either call to find out the name or don't write the letter.

When writing someone you don't know, and whose name gives no indication of gender (such as to Chris Pond, Jan Amos, Pat, or a person with an unfamiliar foreign name), if you have no way of finding out, use "Dear Chris Pond." Such a vocative is not strictly proper, but it is functional, and when "Chris Pond" responds, he or she may give you a hint.

Signing Off

The valediction (adapted from the Latin *vale*, meaning "farewell") is the message used to end a letter. The usual valedictions are "Sincerely," "Sincerely yours," or "Very truly yours."

Others, such as "Regards," "Kind regards," "Fondly," "Best regards," "Best wishes," "With affection," and those that may be even more personal are best reserved for letters between acquaintances, friends, or intimates.

Chapter Three

Public Displays of Etiquette

Dinner Parties

Seating

Dinner parties honoring an individual or couple need not involve a dais (DAY-us) or raised head table. The average home dining room can easily be set to honor a guest. Seating always alternates male and female; the man sits to the left of the woman he escorted.

- *Man and woman host a dinner for 10.*
  Clockwise from top of vertical table:

hostess, male, female, male, female guest
of honor, host (at bottom of table), female,
male, female, male guest of honor.

- *Woman alone hosts a dinner for eight.*
  Clockwise from top of vertical table:
  hostess, male, female, male, female guest
  of honor (at bottom of table), male (acting
  host), female, male guest of honor.

Note that, in each case, the guest of honor
is seated at or near one end of the table, but
never in the center.

Planning the Menu

Professional caterers know to the ounce
how many bottles of wine, how many heads of
lettuce, and how many hors d'oeuvres a function will require based on the time of day,
number of guests, and even season of the year.

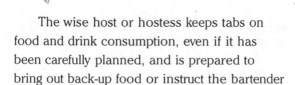

The wise host or hostess keeps tabs on food and drink consumption, even if it has been carefully planned, and is prepared to bring out back-up food or instruct the bartender to pour short shots if inventory gets limited.

Spending Time with Guests

It is the gifted host or hostess who can make each guest feel that he or she is the only one present, despite the size of the crowd. That having been said, it is the selfish guest who tries to monopolize a host's or hostess's time at a large party.

The host or hostess must greet each guest individually and make introductions to those nearby, all the while keeping a sharp eye out for stranded guests and duties that need looking into. Some formal affairs (such as at the White House) specifically provide garrulous people whose sole job is to facilitate introductions and to see that no solo guest is left alone.

Dress

It is mandatory that the invitation to a formal dinner party indicate the dress required. If it should omit such information, the guest may inquire after the mode of dress when accepting the invitation.

For Men. Depending on the time of day and the occasion, formal attire can vary. Gone is the era of cutaway, mourning coat, frock, beach wear, lodge wear, and so on. Those modes may still apply in high society and diplomatic circles, but those that most men are apt to encounter include:

Black tie (this is what is meant when "formal" attire is announced on an invitation). A black tuxedo with black trousers, solid black jacket, a white shirt, and a bow tie are worn. Either a waistcoat (vest) or cummerbund is acceptable. Suspenders (braces) may also be worn instead of a belt; black socks, and solid black shoes are appropriate. Fashion is easing up a bit to allow double-breasted jackets and even colored jackets, although not on strictly formal occasions.

White tie. Attire includes a white tie, a wing collar, a tail-coat, black socks, and solid black shoes. This type of affair is very rare these days; think Fred Astaire.

Semi-formal. Attire includes a white jacket, black or dark trousers, a bow tie, a white or ruffled shirt, a cummerbund, and solid black shoes. Increasingly, all items but the shoes may be selected in colors and patterns.

Business. Attire includes a suit with dress shirt, a full-length necktie, dark socks, and black or brown shoes. (Red neckties are power ties.)

Informal/casual. Business attire or good slacks, a sport jacket, a dress shirt, dark socks, and black shoes are appropriate. A tie is optional the farther west you go.

For Women. Just as no one is supposed to notice a man's attire, *everyone* pays attention to what a lady wears. Women today have far more leeway than in the past; fashion and social change have done wonders in that area. The only point to remember is that a lady's mode of dress should match that of the gentleman escorting her. Here's where to start:

Formal (evening gown to accompany man's white tie). Attire includes a full-skirted dress (off-shoulder if desired), suitable for dancing, length not quite to floor; long gloves reaching to elbow, elegant shoes (heels), and jewelry; and a shoulder wrap if needed. Never wear a hat with an evening dress.

Formal (dinner dress to accompany man's black tie). Attire includes an on-shoulder, mid-calf to floor-length dress; long sleeves, shoulder wrap, and long gloves; elegant shoes (heels); jewelry; and no hat.

Semi-formal. Attire includes a mid-length dress or gown; elegant shoes; and a shoulder or full wrap. Dress attractively and comfortably (low shoes).

Informal. A mid-length dress or pant suit is appropriate.

Business. A mid-length dress or pant suit is appropriate. Suits with jackets are seen as "power" clothes. Dark shoes are worn.

Casual. Whatever.

Arrival Time

Nobody wants to be the first to arrive at a party, but somebody has to be. Local custom, rather than strict etiquette, addresses this thorny topic. Of course, the host or hostess should be prepared by the time of the arrival of the first guest and may even "break the ice" by inviting a few people to "come early so we can spend some time together before the others get here."

However, the person throwing the party has the obligation to be ready at the stated time. Generally speaking, guests for a dinner party should arrive within five minutes of the time printed on the invitation. Guests for cocktails, where a span of time is given, may arrive any-where within it. More pragmatically, other parties begin to boogie half an hour to an hour after the given start time.

Crossed Legs

Ladies over ten wearing dresses are expected to sit with their knees together or their legs discreetly crossed; gentlemen, who presumably wear trousers, may sit however they wish, although allowing one's legs to spread in public is equally rude.

Seeking Professional Advice in Social Situations

Doctors, lawyers, and other professionals are constantly being cornered at parties and asked advice, usually by people who don't want to pay for it. A polite tactic to deflect such encounters is to tell the questioner, "Your problem sounds interesting, but I really can't make a reasoned decision now. Why don't you call me at the office tomorrow and we'll set up an appointment?"

When People Work for You

Salary, duties, house rules, and days off must be established when a household employee is hired. Employment contracts are not necessary, but proper tax and Social Security forms must be completed.

People in service are not lesser life forms who may be abused at will or whim; they are people whose job is to attend to the needs of their employers. They are not invisible and should not be ignored, but allowed to go about their business.

Days off, once established, must be respected. They may also be discussed if both parties are willing, such as if their holiday travel and your holiday entertaining conflict.

It is important to check the references of someone whom you seek to employ, particularly inside your home. Do not be bashful about asking why the applicant left his or her last posi-

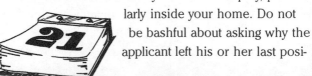

tion, and by all means phone the last employer to confirm the information.

Salaries for household employees vary widely according to the duties required, number of hours, amenities provided, community, and experience. The value of room and board is accounted for in setting the wages of live-in servants, and experienced live-out or part-time servants will probably have a rate already established. Amounts vary by community; consult an employment agency.

Letters of Recommendation

What an employee's letter of recommendation doesn't say may be as important as what it does say.

A perfunctory letter from a previous employer may indicate an uncomfortable parting or unsatisfactory service, but nothing actionable. An effusive letter, on the other hand, may oversell the applicant. Only a phone call will determine what is actually the case.

Restaurant Do's and Don'ts

Making Restaurant Reservations

In most cases one may phone a restaurant on the day a reservation is desired. Give them the number of people who will be attending, the name in which the reservation will be held, and ask any necessary questions: Do they take credit cards? Is there wheelchair access? Do they admit families with children? Can they accommodate someone in your party who has special dietary requirements? And so forth.

Fine restaurants, such as hotel main dining rooms, book tables weeks in advance, especially around the holidays. Phone well ahead of time. Some trendy restaurants think they are so special that they refuse to accept reservations. Go somewhere else.

Canceling Restaurant Reservations

If you find that you are not going to be able to keep your restaurant reservation, call them to release your table. Even if you remember at the exact moment you were due at the restaurant, call anyway.

Restaurants plan on a certain amount of overbooking, to be sure, but that is no excuse to forget your obligation. After all, because you held a table, another patron was turned away. The next time it could be you. (Some restaurants now require a credit card number for a reservation and apply a cancellation fee to no-shows. They are to be avoided—two wrongs don't make a right.)

Arriving at the Restaurant

If you have made a reservation, arrive on time and report to the host or hostess at the door. He or she will check off your name and either show you to your table (if it is ready) or suggest how long you may have to wait. Any wait longer than 15 minutes in an established restaurant is a hint that something is wrong.

The maitre d' may suggest that you have a drink at the bar until your table is ready; the restaurant should buy it if the delay is their fault. (Even if you are "comped" for the drink, you should leave a cash tip for the bartender of 15 to 20 percent of the drink's value).

If It's a Lousy Table

Not all restaurant tables are created equal. Those near the bathroom, kitchen, piano, or busing stations are less desirable than those in quiet corners, or near the window, or with a view.

If you are unsatisfied with your table as you are led to it, ask for a better one—but only if you really want it, not just to show off. Look around to see whether there even *are* any others. If so, are they already reserved? Be prepared to wait if you change because others are in line. Tipping the maitre d' seldom helps you get a better table if there are none available.

Addressing Waiters

Vernacular has begun calling waiters and waitresses *servers*, *waitpersons*, and *waitrons*, all of which are incorrect. Waiters are properly called "waiter," and waitresses are properly called "Miss." Waiters are not called "sir." That's just the way it is. They should never be called *garçon*, which is an insult in America (it means "boy"). The customer also should pay attention to the waiter's face to distinguish him from another table's waiter.

In America, one does not wave or snap one's fingers to get a waiter's attention; it is the waiter's job to notice his tables. If he doesn't, a patron may ask a passing waiter to "please ask our waiter to come over."

Finally, customers who purposely belittle a waiter actually belittle themselves. The proper way to complain about a waiter is to summon the maitre d' and inquire about what the problem is (if there is one, he needs to know about it for everybody's sake).

Disturbances in Restaurants

Patrons who shout, sing, laugh loudly, or toss objects—in other words, who think they're at home—disturb others and ruin the dining experience (unless the restaurant is known for its party atmosphere). If the restaurant manager receives a request from other patrons, it is his or her job to get the noisy party to be quiet.

Children in Restaurants

It is important for parents to expose children to good restaurants so that they may grow up accustomed to enjoying fine food and practicing good manners in public. If the parents cannot get them to behave, they are not welcome.

Parents have every right to bring pouty toddlers and crying babies to "family" restaurants. Customers who wish to avoid children should dine elsewhere or request a seat away from them. A parent whose child misbehaves in a restaurant should leave the room with the child until he or she calms down.

Ordering the Meal

Years ago (and even today in some restaurants) the gentleman was handed the menu with the prices on it, while the lady's menu had none.

Today there is a counterpart: the waiter recites the day's unlisted specials, usually omitting the price. You should not hesitate to ask the prices if it is a concern. The waiter will then take drink orders, bring them, and leave.

The waiter should not be summoned back to the table until each guest is ready to order; when all guests have closed their menus, the waiter knows to approach. Questions about the menu may be asked at this time, as well as inquiries about ingredients, preparation, and so forth. A waiter should be completely knowledgeable about what his kitchen is serving or must offer to find out. Ladies order first. Historically, this has been so that they are not pressured by the gentleman to have what he is having or to have something in the same price range.

Wine

The wine steward, or *sommelier*, can help you choose a wine that is within your price range and that suits the meal. To be sure, some are more diplomatic at it than others.

Generally speaking, you should match the color of the wine to the color of the food: red for meats, white for fish. When in doubt, match a sturdy food with a sturdy wine: chicken and white wine, duck and red wine, and so on. Above all else, though, the wine you like is the wine that's right, and vice versa.

The sommelier will present the chosen wine bottle to the person who ordered it. The routine is as follows: you will examine the label

to confirm that it is correct. The sommelier will then open it and place the cork in front of you. The innermost end of the cork should be moist, which suggests that the wine has been properly stored on its side and no air has gotten in to spoil it.

A small amount of wine will then be poured into your glass. This serves two purposes. One, obviously, is to allow you to taste it. The other is to prevent guests from getting any small bits of cork that may have fallen in when the bottle was opened.

Examine and admire the color and bouquet of the wine. Then taste it (first cleanse your palate with a sip of water or piece of white bread). Don't slurp the wine, just taste it. If it is satisfactory, nod, thank the sommelier, and direct him or her to fill the other glasses. If the wine has spoiled, you may send the bottle back without obligation and request another.

In fine restaurants the sommelier will sometimes appear with a silver cup hanging around his or her neck and will taste the wine first. This means that the sommelier will catch the cork bits, but, more important, that he or she will ensure that the wine hasn't spoiled in shipping or storage (it sometimes does). In such restaurants it is customary for the waiter to refill the glasses.

Refusing Wine. If one does not want wine, one covers one's glass with one's hand when it is offered, or simply says, "No, thank you," when asked. The old custom of turning over one's wine glass so that it cannot be filled is ostentatious and clumsy.

Toasting

The ritual of toasting a guest of honor is as old as the spirits chosen with which to make it. The host offers the first toast. If there is talking, he may quiet the room and gain attention by tapping carefully on the edge of a wine glass (don't try this on fine crystal!).

A toast should be to the point. The person making it stands and raises his wine glass toward the honoree. Other guests merely raise their glasses. When the toast has been made, each guest takes a sip of wine.

Nondrinking guests may raise their empty wine glass, or a glass of whatever else they may be drinking, *except water*. Raising the water glass, or not raising a glass at all, may be construed by some as disapproving the toast. Children may raise their milk glasses. The recipient of the toast sits and

does not drink to himself. He may respond with his own toast. In large dining functions where there is a dais, only those people on the dais may propose toasts.

When the Meal Is Served

The host or hostess does not begin eating until all other guests have been served. The kitchen is supposed to time their preparation so that all meals for a table are ready at the same time. The waiter is supposed to monitor this. If there has been a major delay with one meal, the waiter may offer to bring out the others with apologies to the stranded diner. If the delay is to be more than a few minutes, everybody else should begin.

Complaints about the Food

Waiters in better restaurants never ask, "Is everything all right?" because, if the food wasn't all right, it should never have been brought to the table in the first place. If a patron has a complaint about the meal, he should stop eating and the host should summon the waiter. Others at the table are not required to stop eating. The waiter should remove the offending meal to the kitchen for adjustment or replacement, no questions asked.

Clearing the Place

Because people eat at different speeds, some will finish before others. No plate should be cleared until all diners have finished their meal.

The signal for a finished meal is to leave the knife and fork on the upper-right-hand edge of the plate, in the "10 and 2 (o'clock)" position. Regardless, many restaurants today insist on clearing the table before all parties have finished ("Let me just get these out of your way"). Perhaps they are short of dishes. Perhaps they want to rush you out the door. More likely, they just have bad manners. It also is rude for one patron to ask to have his place cleared ahead of the others in his party.

Doggie Bags

There is nothing wrong with requesting the waiter to wrap an uneaten portion of a meal to take home. After all, you paid for it (at fancier restaurants, the bag is presented to the departing guest at the door).

Reaching for the Tab

The person who asks the waiter to bring the bill is the one who will be expected to pay it, and the waiter should set it before him or her. A waiter who brings the bill without being asked to do so is subtly hinting that he wants you to leave the restaurant. He will usually place it in the center of the table, equidistant from the diners.

The host of a meal should reach for the bill when the waiter brings it, check the addition, and leave payment. Cash or credit card are the usual means of payment, although personal checks and travelers checks are accepted (inquire when making the reservation). Patrons using coupons should inform the waiter at the time they are first seated.

The waiter will return with the credit card slip or cash change, usually with enough small bills to make tipping convenient. Waiters earn the bulk of their income from tips, despite having to report the income to the IRS. Some patrons will charge the meal, but leave the tip in cash, which is a very kind gesture.

Fighting Over the Tab

The person who asks others to dine is the one who pays the restaurant tab and should make this clear at the time the invitation is extended. There is no need for the guest to make a grand gesture of reaching for it or to ask to leave the tip. An offer to reciprocate is always welcome. When a woman invites others to dine, she may have to stress specifically that she does, in fact, expect to pay the bill.

In some communities (particularly Hollywood), people are known to go to extraordinary lengths to pick up a restaurant tab, probably as a tactic to obligate others. Techniques include arriving early and asking the headwaiter to imprint one's credit card; excusing oneself to the rest room and secretly settling at the register; and signing the tab to one's private restaurant account. Legend has it that Marlon Brando once won a check-grabbing contest by threatening his guest, "If you don't let me pay, one of us is going to leave this restaurant naked." It is rude to deprive a host of the privilege of paying for the meal.

Tipping at Restaurants

For table service, a tip of 15 percent of the pre-tax total is an accepted tip for adequate table service; 20 percent is fast becoming the norm, however. It all depends on the level of service. For groups many restaurants automatically add a 16 to 18 percent gratuity for parties of eight or more (the additional points are meant both to reflect the need for more service and to counteract the 3 to 6 percent credit card surcharge the restaurant must pay).

For counter service, 15 percent is adequate (but never less than twenty-five cents). No tip is expected in a self-service restaurant or cafeteria except where someone refills coffee cups or iced tea glasses, carries your tray to the table, or provides personal service, in which case 10 percent left on the table is adequate. Busboys are not tipped (they are tipped by waiters).

Bartenders get 15 to 20 percent. If you have ordered a drink while waiting for a table, you may settle the tab before you leave the bar. If the bartender rolls your tab over into your dinner bill, you should nevertheless tip the bartender before you take your table.

At catered affairs the servers' tip (15 percent) is covered by the contractor, but patrons may leave $1 for a bartender over the course of the evening (not per drink).

A wine steward receives 15 to 20 percent of the cost of the bottle if he has helped you choose the wine, has not tried to force a more expensive one than you wanted, and has seen that your glass was never empty. The tip is paid to him directly in cash as you leave the restaurant. If he has merely taken your order and left you to refill your own glasses, 10 to 15 percent is adequate, paid the same way.

The maitre d' (host) is not tipped each time, although $5 to $20 (depending on the restaurant) slipped to him once in a while is appropriate if you are a regular customer and he gets you an especially good table. Otherwise, a $5 bill is sufficient.

Restaurant musicians get tipped $1 for a special request, and it is perfectly all right to keep eating while it is played, as long as you don't talk through it. Some restaurants have strolling musicians who expect a tip of $1 just to go away. Funny thing is, if you don't pay them a dollar, they still go away.

Coat check is $1 per item, regardless of how many hangers they use. Many checkrooms require advance payment, which is insulting and does little to speed up retrieval.

Parking valet: If there is not a service charge posted at the door ($2 to $5 in most cities), $1 to $2 upon delivery is adequate. Valets are not paid when the car is dropped off (tips are usually pooled). Flamboyant people with expensive cars have been known to tip $20 in advance and ask the valet to use two parking spaces to prevent accidental scratching.

At the Dinner Table

People can tell more about each other's character by their behavior at dinner than by anything else they do. This is where etiquette levels the playing field.

The Dinner Invitation

A formal dinner invitation is typically extended between two and four weeks before the scheduled event. It will include date, time, address, and the name of the host or hostess. It also may include mode of dress and will most likely request an R.S.V.P.

Replying to a Formal Invitation

One must reply immediately, by telephone if the number is given, or in writing if it is not, to a formal invitation. Failing to do so is unforgivable.

The response must be "yes" or "no" (or, in more formal terms, *accepts* or *regrets*). If you want to go but are otherwise committed that evening, you may not break the previous commitment to attend the "better" one. There is no such thing as "I'll come over for coffee and dessert" in formal entertaining. When responding in writing, one should repeat the date, time, and address as it appears on the invitation.

Special Diets

Whether for aesthetic, health, or allergenic reasons, some people must bring their special diets out with them. If one is on a particular eating regimen, one should discuss it with the hostess when accepting a dinner invitation. If she can accommodate the diet, fine; if not, she has no obligation to tailor her entire menu to suit one guest (unless he or she is the guest of honor). It is important for guests suffering from life-threatening allergies (such as MSG or shell-fish) to disclose this to the hostess, who may avoid these substances or alert the guest to skip certain courses.

If a guest does not like what is being served, he or she should accept only a small portion and then ignore it. Vegetarians and those who may be offended by something that is served need not partake of it. One may explain one's reasons to the hostess privately, but should not make a political speech at the table. Guests with even more esoteric eating requirements either should not accept the dinner invitation in the first place or should eat on their own beforehand.

Changing Your Mind

Once you have accepted an invitation, you may not back out at the last minute for any reason short of death or sudden illness. On the other hand, if a compelling out-of-town trip arises, you should notify your hostess as soon as you learn of the conflict and apologize for your impending absence. (Note: there really has to be such a trip.)

Conversely, if you find that you are suddenly available after having sent regrets, you may be out of luck. If it's a large reception, you may be able to call and ask the hostess if you can still come if she has room. For a small gathering with place cards, however, you should resign yourself to staying at home with a good book.

The Extra Man

Single men whom the hostess knows to be unaffiliated should not automatically assume that a dinner invitation issued to them includes a female guest. "Extra men" are socially valuable as such. A hostess may be planning on pairing him (for the evening, but, hey, who knows?) with a similarly single woman. There is an important distinction between an "extra man" and a gigolo: an extra man's duty ends after dinner.

B.Y.O.B., B.Y.O.F., and Pot Luck Dinners

"Bring Your Own Bottle," "Bring Your Own Food," and "Pot Luck Dinner" parties are always thrown among friends. They are wonderfully informal gatherings to which each person brings whatever he or she desires to consume and share.

The notations "B.Y.O.B.," "B.Y.O.F.," and "Pot Luck" have no place in formal entertaining. The hostess or host is expected to provide everything.

Bringing Wine

One does not bring anything to a formal dinner; the hostess will have planned everything and will require nothing beyond your presence. It can, however, be a thoughtful contribution to a dinner among friends to bring the hostess

a bottle of wine. Some bring dessert instead. It is not incumbent upon the hostess to serve the gift if it does not complement the meal she has already planned. It is perfectly proper for the hostess to thank the guest and save the gift for a more appropriate time, e.g., "What a wonderful gift, but I've already opened a bottle, so why don't we enjoy this another time."

To Clink or Not to Clink

Large groups do not clink their glasses during toasts. Individuals (particularly lovers, but anybody toasting a special occasion) may touch their wine glasses together if they wish. Superstition suggests that the glasses be "clinked" at unequal height, never at the same level. If those raising their glasses in a toast are seated too far apart to touch them, the raising itself is sufficient.

Seating Arrangements

The hostess decides who will sit where at a dinner

Mrs. Smith

party. If she does not lay out place cards, she may direct people where to sit. Thoughtful hostesses will write the guest's name on both sides of the place cards so that persons sitting across from each other can read them.

A gentleman will steady a lady's chair while she sits. No gentleman should be seated until all ladies are seated, with the exception of the hostess (if she is serving), who may stand and advise her guests, "Please be seated." Guests must sit where directed.

If the first course is a cold course (such as melon), it will already be on the table. If it is a hot course (such as soup), the hostess should tell her guests, "Please be seated while I get the first course." Guests need not ask if the hostess needs help. If she does, it is her duty to request it ahead of time or make arrangements for it.

Beginning the Meal

Upon being seated, place the napkin on your lap. Napkins do not belong tucked into collars. Remove the napkin completely from the napkin ring if one is used. Only when the hostess or host picks up her or his fork may the other guests pick up theirs.

Buffet Dining

Buffets, or serve-yourself meals, are popular for feeding large, informal groups. Hosts choosing a buffet should provide food that can be easily served, cut, and eaten, preferably on small tables, but usually balanced on laps.

Guests should not fill their plates to overflowing and should be careful not to mix foods or serving utensils on the buffet table. They should also not sneeze on, cough over, or taste selections until they are eating from their own plates.

Seconds

Guests are not offered additional helpings at formal dinners, although individuals may help themselves if platters are passed. A hostess at an informal dinner will not ask, "Does anyone want seconds?" per se, but may offer them spontaneously. If only one person takes some, the hostess should take some more, too. Buffets, of course, are fair game as long as the food lasts. Friends gathered around the table after dessert may continue to pick at the remains. That's what friendship is all about.

Eating Habits

The old joke goes, "Is it proper to eat olives with the fingers?" "No, the fingers must be eaten separately." In truth, some foods *may* be eaten using fingers, others are best savored with forks, and even with sticks.

Despite popular belief, it is *not* automatically permitted to pick up food with bones (such as lamb chops, chicken, or ribs) unless the food is either served at a picnic, in a rib joint, or at some other place where that eating style is encouraged, *or* if the chop has paper wrapped around a trimmed end bone (the "panty"). There are exceptions, however.

Right-Hand-Only Eating

Some Eastern cultures insist that eating be performed only with the right hand. Using the left hand would be an insult, a tradition harkening back to the days when the left hand was devoted to matters of personal cleanliness.

Ethiopian food, for example—a mound of a spicy, succulent stew served in the middle of a large, round bread presented to the group on a platter—is eaten with the right hand. One tears off a small piece of bread, pinches an amount of the food with it, and carries it to the mouth.

Asian Dining

In Chinese, Japanese, Korean, and other Asian cultures, people eat with chopsticks. One should not attempt to use chopsticks unless one is reasonably skilled with them. Chinese dishes are brought from the kitchen when they are ready, and all at the table share them, carrying a serving to their own rice bowls and eating individually from the bowl. It is rude to jam your personal chopsticks into a common dish. You should use the serving spoon or chopsticks provided. Your own chopsticks may be left on the edge of your rice bowl while you are still eating, or rested on the edge of your individual serving bowl or plate when you are finished.

Asian noodle dishes are brought to the mouth with chopsticks. When you bite off the excess, you should be careful not to splash. Larger objects, such as wontons, pot stickers, and dumplings, are brought to the mouth with chopsticks, and a bite is taken from them. Slurping is a sign of appreciation, but don't get carried away.

Sushi (raw or cooked fish on rice cakes) may be eaten by hand or chopsticks, but sashimi (sliced fish alone) is eaten with chopsticks only.

The European Knife and Fork

The custom in America is to hold the fork in the left hand while the right hand, holding the knife, does the cutting. One then lays down the knife, switches the fork from the left hand to the right, spears the food, and carries it to the mouth. One also uses the fork to scoop up peas, corn kernels, and other elusive objects.

The European custom is to keep the fork in the left hand, use the knife to push food onto it, and bring the fork to the mouth. In Great Britain, peas, corn, and other small objects are eaten by squashing them onto the fork for delivery to the mouth. Each version has its advantages. Using one style when the majority uses the other has become entirely appropriate.

The One Exception

It is improper to hold the fork in one's fist and stab the meat with it. The fork is held with the left hand, tines down, left index finger extended along the bridge to steady it.

Cutting Up Food

A diner cuts up his food as it is eaten, not all at once, unless he is doing so for a small child.

Eating from Another's Plate

It is impolite to take food from someone else's plate. If one desires to sample or share food, a small portion may be offered on the bread-and-butter plate.

How Much to Take

When a serving dish is passed around the table instead of the meal being individually plated, one may take what one wishes to eat. Some items are clearly portion-controlled (a breast of chicken, a chop, a baked potato, a fish fillet, etc.), in which case the diner accepts a single one unless the hostess suggests otherwise.

For vegetables or less precise foods (shrimp, stews, etc.), try to see what others are taking. When in doubt, take what appears to be a six-ounce serving (this is standard for restaurants and may be applied to the home). Platters are passed around a table counterclockwise, by the way.

Licking Fingers, Smacking Lips

Food, once it goes into the mouth, should not be seen or heard from again by anybody but the person eating it. Chew with your mouth closed, without talking. If the meal is "picnic style" one may lick one's fingers.

Messy Foods

Ideally, dinner parties feature food that can be eaten with a minimum of fuss. In a perfect world, grapefruit is served already sectioned; shrimp is already peeled; cornish hens are pre-boned; nobody serves chili dogs; and so forth.

In reality, however, if you find you cannot chew something, place it discretely on the side of your plate with your fingers where it won't be noticed.

If you catch a morsel of food between your teeth and cannot dislodge it with your tongue, do not pick at the table, but excuse yourself to the rest room. Should you drip something on your tie, blouse, or pants, you may ask your hostess for assistance. If the splash goes on the tablecloth, say "excuse me" and ask for help.

Clearing One's Place

It is the job of the host or household employee to remove spent plates from the guests. Guests may not push their own plates out of the way. It is improper to clear the table by stacking or passing; each place must be cleared individually. No plate should be heard touching another plate.

Elbows

Yes, it's true, elbows do not belong on the table at a formal dinner. On informal occasions, however, it is perfectly all right to lean forward and relax (once the plates are cleared, of course).

Smoking

No ashtrays means no smoking.

Details, Details

Place Settings

Nothing intimidates dinner guests more than coming face to face with an array of glistening implements, many apparently duplicating each other. This shouldn't happen. No more than three of any kind of implement should be on the table at the same time. And silverware is placed in order of its use. Always remember: *use silverware from the outside in. If in doubt, watch the hostess.*

The exception is when a piece of silverware is in the wrong place. Discreetly use the correct one. Should the guest of honor use the incorrect implement, however, other guests should do the same, as embarrassment is to be avoided, even at the awkwardness of eating prime rib with a shellfish fork.

A basic formal dinner place setting includes, left to right (see illustration): fish fork, meat fork, salad fork; plate; salad knife, meat knife, fish knife; soup or fruit spoon. If there is a shellfish fork it goes to the right of the spoon. *Notice that the cutting edges of all knives face inward, or to the left. The most frequent mistake people make in setting a table is putting the knives on the left of the plate or facing them the wrong way. A helpful rule: place knives so they can be picked up and used as is.*

As coffee and dessert are served after the main course, teaspoons and dessert spoons or forks will not be presented until they are brought with the dessert. The tablecloth in front of the guest must never be exposed. It is set with a large service plate onto which the first course will be placed. The napkin is placed to the left of the forks if the first course

Fish fork Meat fork Salad fork Plate Salad knife Meat knife Fish knife Soup or fruit spoon

is placed on the service plate or on the center
of the service plate if the first course will be
served hot.

Unlike formal meals, informal meals do
not include all the courses, wines, and conven-
tions. Salad and meat forks, a single knife, and
a soup spoon usually are adequate. A water
glass and single wine glass will also do the
job. The napkin is placed to the left.

Glasses

Unlike silverware, drinking glasses are placed in order of height and are used as they are filled, according to the meal: water goblet, white wine glass, red wine glass, sherry glass.

Wine Glasses. Oenophiles differ on the appropriate shape for a basic wine glass, but if there is one all-purpose glass it is one with a tulip-shaped bowl. There is, however, a good reason for having such an assortment of other shapes: tall, narrow, rounded, tapered, small opening, large opening, or fluted. Because the human tongue can receive different sensations (salt, sweet, sour, bitter) at different points on its surface, wine glasses are shaped to deliver a

Champagne

Water goblet *White wine* *Red wine* *Sherry*

particular wine to the specific area of the tongue that can best taste it.

Wine is poured from the right, and the glass is never filled more than halfway. It is raised to the mouth by its stem, not the bowl, to keep the hand from warming the contents.

Red wine, which may contain sediment, can be cradled at an angle in a wine basket and poured that way; either red or white wine may be placed upright in a special collar to prevent drips from staining the tablecloth.

Centerpieces

Nothing is worse than a floral centerpiece so tall that guests opposite each other at the table cannot see past it. However, if a guest has been so kind as to send the centerpiece ahead, it would be an insult not to display it. An unwieldy centerpiece can be displayed, acknowledged, and adored, and then removed gallantly to a sideboard prior to a formal meal service.

Formal Table Service

Professional servers are trained in French service in which portions are lifted from the serving platter, which is balanced on one hand, with the serving fork and spoon held in the other hand. Service is almost always from the guest's left; plates are cleared from the guest's right. As previously mentioned, at no time should the bare tablecloth be exposed before the guest; a plate should always cover it. Replacement silverware is brought as needed.

Holding on to Silverware

The utensils used for one course are removed with the spent dishes for that course. One does not carry utensils from one course to the next. If a guest has mistakenly used the wrong fork or knife, it is cleared without comment along with those that should have been used and replaced with the appropriate clean one(s) for the next course.

Lemons

If lemons are not already wrapped in cheesecloth to prevent seeds and squirts from escaping, one may insert the tines of one's fork into the lemon wedge and squeeze it over the food. This should prevent accidental squirting.

Salt and Pepper

One does not add salt or pepper to food until one has tasted it. Salt and pepper are shaken directly onto the food, not into the palm of one's hand first. The shaker with lots of holes contains salt, and the other the pepper.

Hors d'oeuvres

Crudités (raw vegetables), canapés (food on crustless bread), and hors d'oeuvres (everything else) are finger foods served before the meal to whet one's appetite, absorb alcohol, and encourage conviviality. They are eaten while standing, mingling, or in any case prior to entering the dining room for the formal meal.

If one serves hors d'oeuvres, a waste plate should be conspicuously placed (and replaced) to allow guests to discard shells, toothpicks, and uneaten food.

Bread and Butter

A small plate, placed to the upper left of the dinner plate, is for bread and butter. The small, rounded butter knife will rest on its upper edge at 10 to 2.

One takes a roll or slice of bread from the basket as it is passed and places it on the bread-and-butter plate. One slices a pat of butter from the butter dish with one's butter knife and transfers the pat onto the edge of the bread-and-butter plate. Thereafter, one tears the bread into small pieces and butters each as needed from the small mound on the plate.

Do not butter an entire roll or slice of bread at once, or take butter directly from the common butter plate to the bread.

Soup

The soup spoon is pushed away from you in the bowl, touched briefly to the side of the bowl to deposit excess drops, and then lifted parallel to the mouth. Only if the spoon is small enough may it be placed into the mouth; otherwise, it is emptied silently into the mouth from its side. The last spoonfuls of soup may be savored by tipping the soup bowl away from you and spooning it as before.

Soup bowls should always be served on a plate so that the soiled spoon may be placed on the edge of the plate and not left in the bowl.

Consommé and Bouillon. These are clear soups, sometimes served cold or jellied, and are eaten with soup spoons. If the soup is specifically served in a bouillon cup with handles on the sides, it may be lifted to the mouth and drunk in that manner, when cooled. A spoon may, of course, also be used.

Salad

Salads may be served before the main course (American style) or after the main course and before the dessert (European style). Either way, they should be prepared with the lettuce torn into bite-size pieces. Salads of asparagus, heart of

palm, whole leaves, lettuce wedges, or other items that require cutting by the guest should be accompanied by separate salad knives and forks (see Place Settings).

Caesar Salad. Usually, Caesar salads are dressed and tossed before they are presented on a salad plate. One form of Caesar is presented with whole (or halved lengthwise) leaves of Romaine lettuce, which the guest then holds by the stalk end to scoop up the tangy dressing. It may also be cut with salad fork and knife.

Asparagus

Plain chilled asparagus may properly be eaten with the fingers by holding the bottom of the stalk and dipping, where provided, into dressing. Where the stalks are presented already dressed, a knife and fork are appropriate.

Artichokes

Artichokes are members of the thistle family. They have a tender heart surrounded by a bristle "choke" and outer leaves, the inner tips of which are edible.

An artichoke is eaten by tearing off individual leaves, dipping the inside end into a sauce or dressing, and scraping the tender flesh off with one's teeth. The "heart" is savored last by scooping out the bristles with the knife. Some chefs will thoughtfully remove the choke prior to serving and may also fill the center with the dip. Scraped leaves are discarded neatly on the edge of the serving plate.

Melon

If a slice of melon is not already cut into chunks, then one uses a spoon to scoop out bite-size pieces with one hand while steadying the wedge with the other. Sometimes a wedge of lime or lemon may accompany the melon. It may be squeezed onto the melon if desired.

Bacon

If bacon is crisp enough to shatter when cut, it may be eaten with the fingers, but if it is soft-cooked it is eaten with a knife and fork.

Small Fowl

Legs of squab, quail, pheasant, and Cornish game hens may be eaten with the fingers after the rest of the meat has been removed with a knife and fork.

Peas

Only the Three Stooges eat peas with a knife. Peas should be scooped or speared with a fork.

Other Veggies

Celery, olives, carrots, jicama, and other vegetables presented as crudités on a relish tray may be eaten with the fingers. Vegetables served dressed or within a salad should be eaten with a fork.

Corn on the Cob

Suitable for informal dining, corn on the cob is grasped with the fingertips of both hands. It is buttered, salted, and peppered only a few rows at a time, with the butter pat first brought to the plate from the butter dish, as with bread and butter.

Pizza

If it's soft and runny, use a knife and fork to cut it into bite-size pieces until the remainder of the slice is small enough to pick up by the edge crust. Or you can just say, "Hey, it's pizza," and go for it; etiquette, schmetiquette.

Chips and Dip

Whatever is to be dipped into salsa, dressing, gua-camole, and so on should be dipped in only once. It is inappropriate (and unsanitary) to put something back into a common dip that has been in one's mouth.

Finger Bowls

Following a meal, guests may be pre-sented with a small dish of liquid, frequently with a slice of lemon or a flower floating in it. This is a finger bowl. One does not drink this liquid. One dips the edges of one's fingers into it, one hand at a time, then wipes them dry on the napkin. One may also touch the lips with the liquid to cleanse them.

The finger bowl may signal the end of the meal, although it may also precede the

dessert. Watch the hostess to see whether
she moves her finger bowl aside (making
way for dessert) or keeps it in front her
(that's all, folks!).

Demitasse

A demitasse is half a cup of coffee served
in a half-cup-size coffee cup. It is served with a
small spoon.

How to Hold a Teacup

It is the Western custom to grasp a teacup
by slipping the index finger through the looped
handle and placing the thumb on the top of the
loop to steady it. One does not wrap
one's hand around the cup or lift it
with both hands, as in Eastern cultures, unless one is in the East
at the time, of course.

Tipping

When Your Host Undertips

Not everybody tips at the same level, but sometimes an obvious mistake can be made. If you notice that your host has grossly under-tipped—and if this is a restaurant where you are known or to which you are apt to return—you may *discreetly* leave more money on the table as you leave.

Drivers

Limousine drivers usually have their tip (17 to 20 percent) added to the overall cost of hiring a chauffeured car. Inquire at the time you make the reservation. Remember to make allowances for your driver to take meal breaks when you do. (Some hotels and restaurants make special provisions.)

The Boss

As much as proprietors of barber shops, beauty salons, flower shops, garages, and other businesses grumble about it, customers do not need to tip them as they would employees. Regular customers may give the owner a holiday gift, however.

Golf Caddies

At a club or public course, a caddie is tipped 15 to 20 percent of the worth of the green fee.

Barbers and Hairdressers

A tip of 15 to 20 percent, and in no case less than $1, is adequate for a barber or hairdresser. Separate services performed by manicurists and shampooists should also be tipped another $2, more for unusually good or detailed service.

Skycaps

Uniformed airline personnel who check luggage curbside are colloquially called skycaps. They earn their salary from tips. A skycap should be tipped at least $1 per checked bag, paid at the time he hands over the claim checks.

Delivery Persons

Florists, supermarket delivery people (whether to the door of the house or trunk of the car), the pizza guy, fruit basket people, and telegram messengers get $1 to $3 depending on the number of or weight of the items.

Federal Express, DHL, UPS, and U.S. Post Office delivery people are not usually tipped, but a $10 to $20 Christmas tip for regular service is appreciated.

Apartment Staff

Apartment complexes and condominium associations usually have a "Christmas pool" into which residents contribute a given amount that is split among the workers who have been attending them all year. Other apartment buildings may have a checklist that they will happily provide to residents for individual seasonal gratuities.

If a building employee has been consistently or especially helpful (rehanging curtains, running out for a quart of milk, parking the car, being discreet in certain matters, etc.), a specific gratuity is called for. Cash always is more appreciated than presents—and is certainly better than booze. The following applies:

- *Repairpeople.* If you tip them each time they do work, then $5 to $10 at year-end is fine; if you do not, then $20 is more suitable.

- *Building superintendent.* A resident super is a blessing, and if the super has performed work for you throughout the year, $50 to $75 is not too much to bestow.
- *Door attendants.* A tip of $25 to $50 is appropriate. The high end applies if they've called taxis, carried baggage, walked your pet, or shepherded your kids.
- *Front desk.* A tip of $25 to $40 is appropriate for the day clerk who sorts your mail and $10 to $20 for the night clerk who rings you when your cab arrives.
- *Others* (delivery person, cleaner, paper carrier, etc.): A tip of $5 to $10 per person is appropriate in a large building, $10 to $20 in a smaller building. If you are in a pinch, the building management can make suggestions.

Nursing Home Attendants

As with apartment and condo staffs, the year-round service by nursing home personnel may be rewarded at Christmas by a single donation to a staff fund. Individuals who have a particularly close relationship with a resident may be given a present, but not liquor.

Deportment

Behavior in a Court of Law

One stands when a justice, judge, or magistrate enters the courtroom and stands again when he or she leaves. The bailiff will announce this.

The judge has absolute authority to call, eject, silence, or cite for contempt anyone present. Chewing gum, talking, drawing, tape recording, reading, and even taking notes can be prohibited, and complaining about not being allowed to do so can be met with a contempt citation.

Court Clothes

Those appearing in court to respond to charges should be dressed for the occasion. A full suit for men or long dress for women is not required, but a neat appearance can greatly benefit one's circumstances.

If one has been arrested and detained, a change of clothes may not be possible. Since not everybody is O.J. Simpson, an indigent defendant may be loaned "court clothes" from a supply the jail or courthouse has for such contingencies (like fancy restaurants that keep a supply of ill-fitting jackets and ugly ties). Relatives of defendants may also furnish court clothes.

Curtseying and Bowing

Americans are proud of the fact that they need bow to no one (unless they're acting on the stage, of course, which says something). Because of this, bowing or curtseying voluntarily can be a demonstration of respect, even if the recipient does not realize how un-American it is.

It is never done when being presented to elected officials in this country and need not be done when being presented to visiting royalty. Socially, though, it can be charming (if a little affected).

A bow can be anything from a slight nod of the head to fully bending over from the waist, and from covering the heart with one's right hand to bending and covering one's stomach with one's left hand braced behind the waist. A

Middle Easterner may show respect by touching his forehead, lips, and heart with his hand while slightly bowing. Asians may press their hands together in front while bowing slightly.

Western women curtsey, in which one pulls the sides of one's skirt slightly aside, crossing one's feet while dipping, and also while bowing one's head (it performs better than it describes!). There is no counterpart if the woman is wearing jeans or shorts, but then such attire would not be worn anywhere curtseying might be expected.

Men and women bow to each other at a formal dance, before the lady takes the gentleman's arm to the dance floor, and bow again as the dance ends. A gentleman also may bow slightly with the head when he is presented to a lady and she offers her hand.

Chapter Four

Mind Your Business

It seems that the rate of reported incidents of sexual and racial harassment in the workplace has been falling, proof, according to those who evaluate such data, that office seminars and sensitivity training sessions are working. What a sad state of affairs that it takes organized programs to teach people something they should have learned growing up: awareness of other people's feelings.

Business complicates matters, however. Because of the unequal power between

employer and employee, it is essential to observe decorum at all times. That does not mean that boss and worker of whatever gender combination must treat each other coldly. It just means that an act that someone in management may consider a supportive personal gesture (such as a hand on someone's shoulder) may be taken as an assertion of power by the person attached to the shoulder.

How an office functions inside its walls is no less important than how it conducts itself toward the public. Good manners make good business. But business involves more than politeness. It also uses protocol, tradition, and, yes, even sensitivity—not just to make a bigger or better sale, but also to develop long-term relationships and inspire trust.

Office Issues

The Job Interview

Prevailing wisdom is that if the applicant lets the boss do all the talking during the interview, the more intelligent the boss will think the applicant is and the better chances are he or she will land the job. Nevertheless, job applicants should be prepared to talk. They should research the company prior to the meeting and be prepared to ask questions of their own.

A job interview can be scheduled by phoning the employer, through the company's "human resources" (personnel) department, by sending a resume and cover letter, or by arrangement through a mutual acquaintance. Whatever the means of securing access, the interview is the key part of the hiring process.

The interview itself is an audition, not a first date. The applicant should wear white-collar clothes. Both parties address each other formally and exchange information, primarily about the applicant's previous work experience. Afterward, the applicant should send a letter of thanks for the interview.

The wise employer will hold off making a final hiring decision until she has interviewed all job applicants. Closure is a mark of decency; the employer or an assistant should call or write all the unchosen candidates to advise them that the job has been filled.

The applicant may thank the employer again and ask that his or her resume be kept on file for any future openings. This grace under disappointment may go farther than the original interview in moving the applicant to the top of the pile for next time.

Boss/Administrative Assistant Relationships

Here are some general rules of thumb in working with an assistant:

- A boss should rise when meeting personnel for the first time.
- When a boss and his or her administrative assistant attend a meeting, the boss should, as a courtesy, introduce the administrative assistant to others taking part in the meeting.
- The boss and administrative assistant should come to a mutual agreement on how they would like to be addressed by each other—whether they want to be called by their first name or prefer to be called by a courtesy title (Ms., Mr.) or professional title and their surname.

Mandated Equality

Some companies have policies that state that all employees, of whatever rank, must be on a first-name basis. This represents an attempt to create a more egalitarian and comfortable work environment. You should follow whatever practice is customary in your office or company.

Business Attire

Unless uniforms, safety gear, or work clothes are specifically required (such as for identification, technology, or construction), business attire should be neat and functional, yet comfortable.

Office workers should wear shirts or blouses cut so as not to distract others. Women generally wear pants or skirts that cover their knees while they are seated, and men wear trousers, not jeans. If a jacket and tie are required for a man, it is customary to allow him to hang up his jacket after he has arrived and work in shirtsleeves with his necktie in place. A woman arriving in a suit may likewise shed her jacket.

Shoes should be comfortable and attractive, but running shoes or other sports footwear are not acceptable. People who choose to commute in athletic shoes should keep a pair of "office shoes" at work and change into them upon arrival. Jewelry should be kept to a minimum, especially noisy or showy trinkets.

Some companies, such as restaurants or theme parks, may set their own dress codes, which may require unusual attire. The employee usually does not have a choice in such matters, so if he or she objects, it may be necessary to quit the job.

Punctuality

People are expected to be on the job at, or a few minutes before, their scheduled start time. There is an unspoken custom among office workers that "the first half hour is for me." Employers don't see it this way. If a person is sitting at his or her desk, window, table, chair, or drill press, then he or she must conduct business.

Absence from Work

If you are being paid to do a job, you should be there to do it. Sick pay, vacation pay, leaves of absence, unpaid leave, and other fringe benefits must be negotiated at the time of employment. Activating them once they have been won, however, may be a different matter.

If you know in advance that you are going to be absent, say, for an overnight hospital stay, you should notify your boss as far in advance as possible so that he or she can arrange to hire a temp worker. The company may have a contract with a temp firm, have a pool of fill-in workers, or determine that they can live without you for a short time. If an employee's absences become frequent, it may be grounds for dismissal.

If you discover that you must miss work (accident, flu, family crisis), then either call your boss or contact whomever the company has designated to handle such crises. Whatever the reason for the absence, it is essential that the employee or a designee (parent, child, spouse, etc.) inform the office immediately. Don't just fail to show up.

"Mental Health Days"

Absences on Fridays or Mondays in cases where there is no illness are commonly

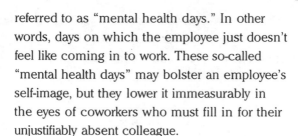

referred to as "mental health days." In other words, days on which the employee just doesn't feel like coming in to work. These so-called "mental health days" may bolster an employee's self-image, but they lower it immeasurably in the eyes of coworkers who must fill in for their unjustifiably absent colleague.

Hygiene

No matter what the job, one should arrive well groomed to perform it. If the job involves contact with the public, it is essential.

Office workers should not wear strong perfume, cologne, or other aromatic scents that may distract or nauseate coworkers. Body odor is both unpleasant and difficult to discuss, and avoiding one permits avoiding the other. Hair, fingernails, and, where applicable, facial hair should be clean and scrupulously groomed.

It is the responsibility of a worker's immediate superior to discuss matters of hygiene with the employee if complaints have been received. If the problem is physiological (such as diet or disease) rather than cosmetic, this should be determined.

Smoking

In many cities, smoking is no longer permitted in public buildings and less and less so in private buildings.

People who smoke tend not to be terribly considerate of people who don't, and this includes not just the subject of second-hand smoke but also the residue that they carry back into the office on their breath, hair, and clothing. On the other hand, nonsmokers, empowered by the medical and moral facts, tend to be equally inconsiderate of smokers.

Etiquette suggests that smokers smoke where smokers smoke and nonsmokers mind their own business.

Making Coffee

Only if making coffee is within an administrative assistant's job description when he or she is hired must he or she do so. If an assistant is not present when a group of managers wants coffee and the person who scheduled the meeting did not have the foresight to order it from a caterer, then the managers can call a break to go out and get some. If the group decides to work through a lunch break and needs to send out for food, the

administrative assistant of the hosting manager may be summoned to make arrangements. Needless to say, it is not the automatic job of any female manager present to "go fetch."

The Office Kitchenette

Offices that have sinks, microwaves, drink machines, refrigerators, and hot plates usually have the problem of coworkers who soil the facilities and do not clean them up.

Unless such janitorial duties are specifically in the job description, every coworker should clean up after himself or herself or set a schedule to take turns doing it. The polite (and astute) manager notices such things and should take the initiative.

Politeness to Administrative Assistants

Politeness to all people is a business rule; politeness to administrative assistants should be a commandment. Although the boss holds the power, the boss's assistant generally has the key to where the power is kept. Befriend them and you've got priority access; alienate them and you might as well take a number—a high number—and wait.

It may feel good to yell at an administrative assistant if the boss has made you angry (if abuse of power turns you on), but it is both rude to the assistant and ineffective. Losing one's temper is never acceptable, but it is even less acceptable to take it out on someone who isn't responsible for the problem and can't do anything about it anyway.

Customer Service

The worker who receives a customer complaint should show his or her manners by remaining polite. If the customer becomes abusive, the worker is under no obligation to endure it and may hang up (if on the phone) or walk away, in each case saying, "It is not my job to be treated in this manner."

As for unwanted phone calls, a polite but firm refusal is always the best way to nip them in the bud, before they escalate. Beyond that, the police may be consulted.

Appointments

The Business Appointment

When two or more people wish to get together in person, they must agree on a time and location. It can be more complicated than it sounds:

- Both parties must agree on the location. Usually the "seller" goes to the office of the "buyer," which produces the perception that whoever goes to the other's office will be at a disadvantage.

- If two parties meet for lunch, the restaurant should be acceptable to both. People who "do" frequent business lunches should be familiar with a variety of restaurants near their place of business. The person who suggests lunch or does the inviting is expected to pay.

- Both parties should write the information in their office appointment books so that they or their administrative assistants don't make conflicting appointments.

- If the appointment is more than 48 hours away, it should be reconfirmed the morning of the day it is scheduled to take place.

- You should always advise your office where you will be and how to reach you when you leave for an appointment.

- Unless it is established in advance, it is improper to bring along additional people to a business lunch.

Persons should arrive for an appointment a few minutes, but never more than five minutes, ahead of time to allow for parking, security clearance, or just getting lost finding the office or restaurant. If the meeting is at an office, the visitor should check in with the receptionist or administrative assistant of the person he is there to see. If there is to be a minor delay, the guest should be offered coffee or other refreshment and asked to wait. A delay of more than five minutes is rude and should be explained.

Handshakes

A firm (not tight or lingering) handshake is the accepted greeting in America. Hugging and kissing is not, except between intimates.

Individuals who because of health, disability, or neurosis cannot shake hands should offer their guest the courtesy of an explanation.

Ending Meetings

If the planned business of a meeting has been concluded, the meeting itself is over. The person running the meeting signals this by standing and offering her hand to the guest, by relaxing and thanking the guest for coming by, or by rising and showing the guest to the door. In some cases the administrative assistant may help the boss end a meeting by entering the room on cue. If there was not sufficient time to conclude the business, another meeting may be scheduled. It is never appropriate to leave one meeting for another meeting before it is over unless this has been made known to all parties in advance.

Keeping Business Appointments

Keeping appointments is sacrosanct. If the appointment must be changed, it is a courtesy to do so well in advance. Often one change can create half a dozen counterchanges, not to mention ill will.

Keeping Professional Appointments

Doctors, dentists, and others who earn their living by office visits may have a policy of charging clients who fail to show up for a scheduled appointment.

These are frequently the same professionals who run late themselves and keep patients stacked up in their waiting rooms. Then there's the story of the $450/hour lawyer who sued a doctor for keeping him waiting—and collected.

If a patient has to cancel a doctor's appointment, courtesy demands that he or she do so at least a day ahead of time to allow the doctor to fill the slot with someone else. Likewise, the doctor's office should advise patients if they are running late, just as a patient should phone ahead to check the same thing. Courtesy works both ways. It is never acceptable for a patient not to show up.

Phone Manners

Business calls should be brief, well organized and businesslike. Callers should identify themselves to whomever answers. If it is a receptionist, they should ask for the person to whom they wish to speak. If they do not know the proper person to handle their request, they should ask for guidance from the receptionist (this is why automatic, prerecorded operators are such bad business).

Once callers are put through to the appropriate office, they should identify themselves. In most cases, the receptionist or an assistant may intercede and "screen" the call, asking for more information if the caller is not immediately known.

Should the recipient wish to speak to the caller, he or she will accept the call. Callers should then reintroduce themselves and immediately explain the reason they are talking. The rest is personal skill.

Personal Calls at Work

Although personal calls are unavoidable as long as human beings work in offices, they should be held to a minimum not only to keep the phone lines clear for important business calls but also so as not to disturb busy (or nosy) coworkers.

Conference Calls

Ganging a large number of people onto the same telephone line can be a time and distance saver; the trick is to juggle everybody's schedule so it can happen.

The highest-ranking member of the proposed teleconference is the one whose schedule must be accommodated, even if she is not the person who suggested the call. Subordinates are expected to rearrange their schedules to oblige.

Flowcharts, spreadsheets, and other visual items should be mailed or faxed in advance to all participants, especially in situations where everybody must share reference. Sending an agenda and participant list is also courteous so people know with whom they are talking.

Speaker Phones

Unless one party has a physical reason
for doing so, it is rude to conduct a conversation on a speaker phone. If there are several
people in the room, everybody's identity
should be disclosed.

Call Waiting

Call waiting is based on the belief that
your next phone call may be more important
than the one you're on. It is equal parts convenience and rudeness. If you have call
waiting that you can deactivate, do so before
phoning someone else.

If you are expecting a call, don't phone
someone else before it comes. If you are
expecting a call but still must phone
someone else or are expecting a call
when someone else calls you first, tell him
or her early in the conversation, "I'm

expecting a call; if it comes, I'll have to call you right back."

If a call comes in while you're talking with someone else, ignore it and hope that the other party calls you back later (unless your local phone company has "caller ID" or "call return"). If you can't bear not knowing, tell your caller, "Excuse me, I have another call. Let me check, and I'll stay on the line with you." Then click, tell the interrupting caller that you'll call her or him back, and return to the original caller.

Screening Calls with an Answering Machine

Whether at home or in the office, people who use their answering machines to screen calls send others the message, "Sometimes I just may not want to be bothered talking to you." It may be efficient, but it is also rude.

Cell Phones

Cell phones can be an annoyance when used inappropriately. But they're also useful for calling ahead to tell your next appointment that you're caught in traffic or to ask driving directions while on the road. If you call someone's cellular phone, keep the message brief because the recipient pays for it. People who use cell phones should always remember that conversations on them are not private and may legally be monitored—by anyone. It's inconsiderate to whip out a cell phone in a restaurant or other subdued public place.

Solicitations

Home Sales

Before people began dwelling in cities where all the necessities of life (except space) were near at hand, they obtained items they could neither grow nor make themselves from peddlers hawking their wares from place to place.

The modern equivalent of this trade, now that door-to-door salespeople such as the Fuller Brush man or the Avon lady have been ousted by chain stores, is the "home sales party."

Popularized by Tupperware® and adapted by firms as wide-ranging as cosmetics, rubber stamps, home repair items, vacation homes, and marital aids, at-home sales parties are a way for friends to exploit each other even away from the office.

If your checkbook and you are invited to one of these commercial parties at a friend's house, the implication is that you should buy *some-thing*—and, by the way, do you have any friends you could invite to next week's party?

As with office collections (see below), no one should be forced to come to, or buy at, such a shamelessly manipulative occasion. "No, thank you, I really don't see anything I need" is a legitimate excuse for those who do not want to buy.

The "Non-No No"

Nobody wants to say "no" in business. It carries a stigma. But sometimes it is unavoidable. Some businesspeople have devised a way of never saying "no" by making it impossible for the other person to say "yes." This is called the "Non-no no." Here's how it works: Say you don't want to accept a job, but at the same time you don't want to get a reputation for declining work. So you ask for a salary so high that you know they'll never pay it. This is tantamount to saying no, except you didn't say no. Moreover, if they can't meet your salary requirement, they haven't said no either. Of course, if they *do* agree to give you the money you want, you have to work for them. So always ask for enough to make it worthwhile.

Office Collections

In larger offices it is not uncommon (in fact, it is a downright regular occurrence) for coworkers to be asked to contribute to each other's causes. These can include birthday parties for colleagues or the boss, betting pools, political and religious donations, funeral and marriage flowers, church and school raffles, sons and daughters selling greeting cards, seeds, wrapping paper, or candy, or even a needy colleague's upcoming rent. Refuse and you're a sour puss; succumb and you're out good money.

It is never proper to solicit a contribution from a coworker. If a coworker wishes to make a donation, he or she should do so privately and without even the slightest coercion.

Although a company should have a stated policy that there shall be no collections of any kind, in point of fact they are impossible to stop. An employee who wishes to decline may say, "I'm afraid my paycheck is accounted for, but if you'll let me know where I can send something in the future, I will see what I can do" or "This is a good cause, but I already have a number of causes I support, so I'll have to pass on this one. Thanks for asking."

That may not do the trick, especially if it's the boss's kid whose school is selling the raffle tickets. Workers pressed into making such buys have been known to write off their expenses and then let the boss explain it to the accounting department. Most simply grin and bear it.

Politics on the Job

There is more likelihood that employees will be asked to make a political donation than a religious one and more chance that they will be held accountable for their response.

Government workers, in particular, are often hit up to support the boss's electoral candidate or the political patron who is responsible for their agency's funding. Even private firms that bid on government contracts have not been immune to this kind of coercion.

Regardless of the illegality of such arm twisting, it persists. One way to discourage the practice is to ask the person making the collection to give you a written bill stating specifically what the donation is for so that you can deduct it from your taxes,

and then offer to write a check. If that signal is not clear enough, you are dealing with a coercion level that transcends etiquette, not to mention the law.

Prayer at Work

Just as some businesses provide fitness or quit-smoking programs for their employees, some companies may hold prayer services. If attendance at any such activity is truly voluntary, that is, if no employee is even subtly pressured to attend, there is no problem.

Unless it is an avowedly religion-based company, prayer that is forced on unwilling employees on the job during business hours should be considered an intrusion into their personal lives and thus a violation of manners. On the other hand, where a few employees desire to pray together—say, grace before meals, or a prayer service outside of office hours—

friends who do not join in should maintain respectful silence for the brief observance.

Gifts and Entertaining

Office Parties and Retreats

It may sound odd to link together the office party, which is a celebration, and the office retreat, which is where management and labor share their innermost feelings. However, both gatherings can turn into minefields—and usually do.

The person with whom you share your intimate thoughts after hours can, and probably will, be the one you will have to face on Monday morning. Fortunately, the '60s ethic of hiring "facilitators" to run "T-groups" held in "seminar centers" so that coworkers "can get in touch with their feelings" has fallen out of favor. No employee should be required to attend any function outside of business hours, but office politics are such that no rule covers this intrusion.

Business Gifts

Traditionally, at Christmas, companies and individuals may find it to their advantage to give a gift to someone who has served them well. There is another term for this: *payoff*. This may take the form of items, frequently of great worth, delivered to a person's home or office.

Many companies have strict rules about what, if anything, their employees, particularly those in decision-making positions, may accept from those who may benefit from those decisions. Gracious employers, upon receiving edible gifts (fruit, candy, cookies, etc.), may lessen the obligation by sharing them with their employees.

Business Entertaining

Occasionally, it is appropriate to entertain clients away from the office and outside of office hours. However, restraint is always safe protocol. The hosts' behavior reflects not only on themselves but also on their company. Some courts have held the company legally responsible for the actions of their employees while representing the business. In brief, nothing should take place in the course of business entertaining that could not take place in the office.

Netiquette

Regardless of its newness, the Internet has developed its own set of rules, called, fittingly enough, "netiquette," to govern the way people treat each other in cyberspace.

SHOUTING

To the rest of the world, capital letters are just capital letters, but in the world of netiquette they are shouting, and shouting is very rude. Perhaps because all caps are harder to read, or perhaps because in a medium that relies on words, capital words stand out, people who use them are first warned, then shunned. Or are they *virtually* shunned?

Staying on Subject

Nothing is more distracting than someone who tries to change the subject in an Internet chat room. If you log onto a specific subject room, you have promised to stick to the topic being discussed. If the people in that chat room wanted to discuss something else, they would leave and find another chat room.

Freedom of Speech

Although pressure groups have gotten Congress to pass laws limiting freedom on the Internet, the courts have thus far sided with the First Amendment. Yet freedom of speech and tasteful speech can be different things, and anybody libeling anybody else on the Internet can still be hauled into court. Just because you're typing alone in a room doesn't mean that the whole world isn't watching.

Flaming

Flaming is the (usually) irrational criticism of another person's post. This can be done individually or as a pack, and it is usually way out of proportion to the original post.

Spamming

Named after the Hormel Corporation's famous mystery meat product, Spam®, *spamming* is the cyberspace term for mass mailings of commercial advertisements, most of which are get-rich-quick scams. The term is also used to describe similar material cross-posted to numerous newsgroups. At the risk of stating the obvious, spamming is considered to be extremely poor netiquette.

Spam's most annoying feature is that it is often followed by more spam, which is usually a series of aggravated netizens spamming back replies expressing their lack of desire to receive these unwanted junk e-mails and Usenet postings. When flaming a spammer, remember to not "reply to all," lest you become a spammer yourself.

Anonymity

Because the Internet is private, one never knows whom one is meeting online.

One should extend the same courtesy and caution on the Internet as one would to someone one meets on the phone, in public, or in a dark club: *be careful!*

Cyber Stalking

Just as celebrities and ex-lovers are occasionally stalked by people who cannot leave them alone, so it has become possible to stalk someone on the Internet.

This involves making repeated calls to someone's server, leaving endless messages on his or her e-mail, posting information about the person, scanning photographs (often digitally altered) into the system, and hacking into phone records and other accounts. Tragically, the first Internet murder has occurred: a man drew a woman into a personal meeting by chatting with her online, and killed her.

The same laws that apply to telegraph and telephone fraud apply to the Internet, although only within the United States. Prohibitions against cyber stalking across international boundaries, now as easy as calling next door, are less enforceable.